THE BABA DOWNSTAIRS

THE BABA DOWNSTAIRS

THE LIFE STORY OF A
A MISFIT INDIAN SAINT

THOMAS K. SHOR

CITY LION
PRESS

ISBN: 9781957890685

Your duty is to be, not to be this or that.

—Ramana Maharshi

CONTENTS

CHAPTER 1

IN WHICH THE SCENE IS SET

I

Even before we agreed that Vikram would tell me his life story in an organized fashion so I could write it, in fact at our very first meeting, when he handed me a book he himself had written, I had a feeling almost like déjà vu. It wasn't quite a déjà vu in that I did not feel as if I'd been in that situation before. It was even stranger, as if I'd entered a scene I'd sometimes imagined as an opening scene for an as-yet unwritten piece of fiction.

Though I mainly write stories based on real people and events, I do occasionally have ideas for a piece of fiction swimming around in my head. Some of them never go beyond the state of idle daydream. Others I put to paper and work on from time to time. Sometimes they develop into something; sometimes they go away.

One persistent scene I've sometimes imagined is an encounter between the narrator of the story—a probably only slightly veiled me—and an older man. Something marks out their meeting, perhaps a coincidence, which singles out the one for the other and lends to the encounter a significance beyond just two strangers meeting, as if some purpose was lurking in the background.

In the course of their encounter the younger man comes to realize the old man is not ordinary, but seems to be a man who knows by experience that for which many strive. It's as if he'd actually stumbled upon some kind of a modern-day sage.

Usually, the imagined encounter occurs in some city, perhaps in Europe, in a park by a river, maybe on a sunny Sunday afternoon. When they are about to part, the old man takes from his bag a book and gives it to the younger man. Then they part, never to see each other again.

When the narrator gets home, he looks at the book and realizes it was handmade and probably the only copy in existence. It is a record of the old man's life, a chronical of his experiences, and it holds the key to his unusual understanding.

I never jotted the idea down, let alone wrote the story with this scene at its core. This is because I never filled in the tremendous gaps—such as what was contained in the book. It was just a scene with an atmosphere that returned to my daydreaming imagination from time to time, an old man imparting the gift of his wisdom in such a way.

Now we come to the story contained in the following pages. None of the particulars of my imagined encounter match, yet there is something uncannily similar in the essentials. Dreams have a way of grasping a situation in symbolic form. What is missed in the specifics is captured in the essence. Life can sometimes also take on this quality we call dreamlike when things line up in a meaningful way. That is rather how my encounter with Vikram occurred.

I've often wondered just how stories come. While it is true that my antennae are out—still, it sometimes seems the stories come looking for me. I say this only half in jest. At the very least, an interesting dynamic sometimes comes into play. In this case I didn't go in search of anything; it was Vikram who moved in downstairs, and at the beginning I tried my best to avoid him.

II

First let me set the scene. My wife, Barbara, and I have kept a home in the Himalayan foothills just south of Kashmir for the past twelve years, at which we spend a good chunk of our time living quietly and writing. We have the upstairs of a sprawling mud, stone, wood, and slate roof house built in the 1940s by a well-to-do local family. It has three-foot-thick walls and wooden floors and a lot of crumbling beauty. The house has multiple gates and entrances and verandas set around two courtyards. Though situated in the middle of the village, it is surrounded by terraced fields in which the caretaker tethers his cows and, according to the season, has small patches of corn, wheat, and vegetables. This buffer insures that there are few distractions; therefore, it is a perfect place for my wife, an anthropologist, and I to write.

While at other times of the year we have other commitments and are quite social, we come to this Himalayan village for many months at a time. We live quietly with little to disturb us, dividing our time between writing and taking long afternoon walks into the steep wooded mountains above the village.

Our landlord lives far away. Apart from the caretaker and his wife and young daughter, who live on the other side of the back courtyard, we have had the place mostly to ourselves. Occasionally, during the twelve years that we've been coming there, our landlord has rented out two collections of rooms downstairs, usually only for a month or two at a time. Sometimes these people disturb our peace, sometimes not. Regardless, we naturally prefer it when the house is empty and we have the place to ourselves. Then we can live with our windows wide open to the mountain silence, punctuated only by the sounds of birds and cows, sheep, and when school is out the sounds of distant children at play.

So perhaps you can understand our initial dismay when Vikram moved in. Before we even laid eyes on him, we heard him—loud and clear. His was a voice that could cut right through the thickest stone walls. As he passed beneath us, we could hear that he was Indian, but not local since he was speaking to the caretaker in Hindi, not the hill dialect particular to this part of the Himalayas. His normal voice, it seemed, was loud as another man's yell. This did not bode well.

About an hour after things had quieted down and it seemed he had settled in, the silence was broken by the sound of our front door being violently shaken. Somebody was trying to force it open, and it could be none other than our new neighbor.

Barbara and I work at opposite sides of the L-shaped upstairs of the house. We joke that she is in the West Wing and I'm in the East. We met in the middle, at our violently rattling door, a double wooden door such as you find in these older houses. It opens out from the middle directly onto the top of a steep and narrow wooden staircase. Carefully, we unlatched the doors and opened them just a crack, for he was standing on the narrow top stair pressed up against the door with his hands still tugging on the handles. We didn't want to swipe him off.

We told him through the closed door to back down a few steps so we could open the doors enough to speak. Apparently he understood, for he complied. Because the stairs were so steep, his head was almost on level with our feet. His hair was white and disheveled, his chin showed many days of neglect, and he looked startled. He seemed a bit confused by our sudden appearance so high above him. One hand was clutching the wooden banister. The other was pressed against the opposite whitewashed wall to steady himself. His breath was labored from the exertion of climbing the staircase, which was almost as steep as a ladder.

Though now quite old, and obviously not in great health, he was large and one could imagine he had once been powerfully built. Sputtering something in a mix of Hindi and English about the rooftop and wanting to get a view of the surrounding mountains, he must have realized—as I'm sure we made clear—that there was no rooftop view and that this was our home and therefore a private space. I'm afraid to say we didn't give him much time for his faltering apology. Since it looked as if he was going to resume his ascent into our front room at any moment, we pulled the door shut, renewing our vow to have nothing to do with him. He could easily spoil our peace.

III

Ours is the last village before the foothills give way to the high mountains. The steep uninhabited wooded slope above the village yields to ever higher peaks, beyond which are the razor-sharp snowy peaks and glaciers of the Himalayas proper. Most late afternoons we quit our desks and climb into this forest or up the tight ravine through which the river flows from the heights. The only others we see up there are usually a few of the older folks grazing their goats.

As I said, the house has multiple courtyards and exits. To get to the forest we have to leave the house by way of the back

veranda, off of which are a couple of rooms, which were now occupied by Vikram.

When we opened the screen door to the veranda, which runs
along a good portion of that side of the house, Vikram was walking back and forth across its length. His hands clasped behind his
back, his pace slow and measured, it looked as if he was meditat-
ing—or doing laps. His eyes were trained on the ground before
him, as if he were deep in thought, so deep that he didn't seem to
notice our arrival, even though we let the screen door slap shut
behind us.

It wasn't until he turned that he noticed us.

"Hello," he called out. And in perfect—though uncomfortably
loud—English he introduced himself as Vikram Singh. He told
us that he was from the Punjab, and that he would be staying
through the monsoon.

"For the last years, I've preferred to absent myself from my
life back home for a few months every year. I leave my home and
I don't tell anyone where I'm going. That way I cannot be dis-
turbed. I go during the monsoon. I prefer to be in the mountains
when it rains. I find it peaceful. Maybe one year I'll truly retire
from the world. I'll simply disappear and not return when the
rains are over. That would keep them guessing!"

Vikram laughed, and it was somehow impossible not to laugh
with him.

"The caretaker told me you were a writer," he said, taking on a
more serious tone. "I too have written a book." He rocked his head
Indian style to add emphasis to this fact. He looked me deeply in
the eye. "This book took me twelve years to write. Who knows?
Maybe you will find it interesting."

When I asked him what it was about, he didn't respond. He
didn't even seem to register the question. Then I got it. I understood why his voice tended to be unnecessarily loud: he was deaf,
or perhaps nearly so.

On a windowsill next to his door was the book in question,
a paperback, on the ready, I suppose, for this very moment. He
handed it to me and told me I may keep it. I was slightly taken
aback. I had hardly just met the man, and it appeared to be his
own well-traveled copy. It was badly dog-eared and had various

phone numbers and who knows what little notes and address-
es written in Punjabi on the title page and on the inside of the
covers. It looked as if he had been carrying it around for years.
The book itself was written in English. The cover, which was so
creased from time and travel that I could hardly make it out,
depicted planets floating in deep blue interstellar space. It was
called *A Grain of Truth*. I took it and thanked him. The sun was
not long to setting, so we didn't have much time for our walk.
Slipping it into the backpack with the water bottle, we continued
on our way.

When we got home, I made myself a cup of tea and sat down
with the book. Though he called it *A Grain of Truth*, I quickly
surmised it was some kind of Theory of Everything. It had complicated diagrams, some of them hand-drawn, with captions about
the various forms of infinity, about the 'Actual,' 'Virtual,' and
'Spiritual' worlds. I started reading here and there, but found it so
dense I wondered whether I'd have the patience. I'm not usually
one to go in for these big theories. It was published by some pub-
lishing house in London I'd never heard of. I tried reading here
and there, but it was thick. It looked in need of a good edit. The
quality of the printing and the layout were not particularly good.

I turned to Chapter 1, which opened by saying it might be pre-
sumptuous of him to put his thoughts down in a book since he was
"neither a writer nor a philosopher, a mystic nor a scientist." This
confession, together with the fact that he was obviously present-
ing some sort of Theory of Everything, lowered any expectations
I might have had. Somehow I got distracted, and got no further.

The next day, I was taking the compost bucket outside to
give some pea shuckings to the cows. Again, Vikram was pacing
steadily if slowly across the wide veranda at the back entrance to
the house. Evidently feeling the need to explain why he was pacing back and forth every time I came down, he told me he had, as
he called it, a 'heart defect' that tended to cause his heart to 'mal-
function.' Being at an advanced age, even this slow and measured
pacing was about all he could handle.

Monsoon at our altitude can be quite cool, and it had been
raining. He was wearing plastic chappals and was dressed in
wide-fitting kurta pajamas. He was wrapped in a brown Kullu

shawl. He told me it was a kind of meditation for him, to slowly walk back and forth across the veranda.

He explained that some two or three years back he had had a pain in his chest and was rushed to the hospital where he was told he needed immediate emergency bypass surgery. He didn't follow the doctor's instructions. In fact, he just went back home, threw out the medicine the doctor had prescribed, and never went for the surgery. Though he had had further episodes, he hadn't seen a doctor since.

When he made clear just how precarious his condition was, he did so with a certain wink of the eye, a little sparkle, a glint, as if he were making a point—a *philosophical* point—saying he did not resist but actually embraced the possibility of his imminent and sudden demise, as if it added acuteness to his perceptions. One had the sense he was somehow saying one mustn't hold much importance to such things.

He seemed a man unusually sure of his place in the world, as if he once had held a position of importance. You can tell it from the way some people occupy space. I could well imagine he was retired from some important post, but his demeanor suggested something more. Perhaps he had left it all behind. His hair was a bit long and wild, as if he hadn't seen a barber in some time. Little droplets of moisture had condensed on it. It looked as if it had been knotted by the wind.

I knew well the rooms he was renting—a first room with windows to the back garden, a dark bedroom, and a simple bathroom. They faced north, received no direct sunlight, and were damp. Not the place you'd choose for spending the monsoon.

He asked whether I had read his book, and I told him I had been busy and only had time to glance at it, but that it looked intriguing. I had to say something. It was difficult to tell whether he could hear any of what I said or whether he got it by lipreading, but he seemed to get the gist of it.

A thunderstorm was brewing on the mountain, and I had hoped to complete my little errand with the compost before it hit. I told him that I'd be back but I had to go to the cows before the rain. He did not hear me—or chose not to. So I stood there with the overflowing compost bucket, the bank of swiftly moving cloud darkening the sky, and the cows waiting in the field.

He cleared his throat and began speaking. I had the feeling he had been thinking about what to say. "I wanted to speak to you about my book," he said. "I am well aware that it is difficult in places, and probably incomplete. Still, I believe that beneath its exterior faults it contains at least a kernel of truth. That is why I called the book *A Grain of Truth*." He said this with a touch of irony. He even laughed, exposing a set of brilliantly white teeth. Despite his problems ordering his thoughts with the written word, his spoken English had a self-assurance about it. It also seemed he had an agenda.

He paused. This time I didn't even try to interrupt. It was a strange situation, to say the least. Because he was deaf, or nearly so, in his presence I was effectively mute. I could speak, but since there was nobody there to hear, what was the use?

He was collecting his thoughts, looking out over the wooded hills rising out of the mist.

"Even if I were a writer," he said, "and able to produce a beautifully written book, I wouldn't expect most people these days to understand it."

I gestured the question why. He seemed pleased I was so quick to accommodate his hearing.

"It is because these days most people are hypnotized by a certain mode of thought that is both dominated *and* limited by pure rationality, by the scientific way of seeing. It originated in the West, but I'm afraid it has now infected the East as well. It is a worldwide phenomenon, a mark of our age."

He was silent for a moment and gave me a peculiar look, as if sizing me up. I had the feeling he was deciding whether I was one of the hypnotized, or whether I was capable of understanding what he wanted to say next.

He made a gesture that encompassed the mountains shrouded in mist, the house, and the two of us. Then he continued in a softer tone, as if taking me into his confidence. There was a look of childlike wonder in his aged eyes. "Look around at our world," he said. "Everything we see follows certain natural laws, the laws of nature. Watch how water condenses into clouds and rises up from the valley. See the rain falling to the earth. Feel the wind, the weight of your body on the soles of your feet. Knock your fist on a wooden table to feel something solid. Watch how water flows. See it all by the light of the sun. Consider the myriad stars and galaxies. Physicists have examined the universe, from the subatomic to the inter-stellar, and they have reduced it to the interplay of four basic forces or energies—gravity, the electromagnetic, the strong nuclear force, and the weak nuclear force. Isn't that fantastic? The whole workings of the universe can be understood by only four forces!

"Now they are looking for the Grand Unified Theory that will reduce the four forces to the one behind them. Yes, they hope to account for everything in a single equation. With this, they believe, they will have the ultimate key, that which lays bare the underlying workings of the entire universe. Even Einstein spent his later years searching for an equation that would reduce those four forces to one.

"But I don't believe they will ever succeed, not by following the road they're on. You only have to read what the physicists say about their coveted Grand Theory—that elusive single equation that will explain it all, from the microcosm to the macrocosm, from the subatomic to the intergalactic—to see that for them it is like the quest for the Holy Grail. It arises from the same longing that has dogged humanity from the beginning, the longing for something ultimate, a final word, an ultimate understanding. They hope to clothe in mathematical symbols that which in earlier times was clothed in theological or philosophical terms. The physicists are looking for the mathematical equivalent to the Biblical I AM."

A gust of wind rode up the valley and swirled around us. Vikram looked me deep in the eyes. "The quest has always been the realization of this unity. You can't learn how to realize it. Nobody can teach you to see the underlying unity behind all the division and separation of what we in the East refer to as the 10,000 things. It is acquired in a different manner than the acquisition of any kind of knowledge. The quest for this unity, for this understanding, is unique, and it always has been. It will not conform to mathematics, theology, or philosophy. It will always slip out of your fingers if you grasp after it. It is that which lies beyond. You either get it or you don't. There is nothing incremental about it. No amount of piling up of knowledge or facts will get you there. It would be like trying to build a tower to reach the sky. No matter how high your tower, the sky would always be above you, it would always be beyond your reach. Science is based on knowledge that builds over time. We speak of the progress of science. And it has been tremendous. One can only wonder at the incredible advances in science that we've seen.

"But couldn't it also be true, as mystics have proclaimed from the beginning, that certain things can only be known as a whole, and come to one in a flash, that there are certain shifts of perspective that no piling up of facts or knowledge can ever reach, insights that come not by education and the building up of knowledge upon knowledge, but come as a tremendous ah-ha, ready-made, complete, and self-evident, due to an experience? Maybe we could call it intuition, an immediate cognition or spiritual perception. What the mystics have by direct experience can never be found by plodding reason. No equation can ever encompass it. Sometimes there are great leaps involved, quantum changes, flashes of insight. Even in an individual's life. Just think of falling in love!

"That book I gave you, it took me twelve years to write. It was the result of a transformation I underwent, an experience I had—and an insight I gained—that almost cost me my life, quite literally. I had to wrestle it from the very depths of my being. I nearly died in the process.

"Sometimes something has to dissolve before something new can be born. I'm talking not just about an accumulation of knowledge or a new theory, but a transformation as the result of experience. This is how you affect a quantum jump in your understanding. Neither learned nor taught, this can only be known by direct experience. No equation will ever encompass it. And it is only once experienced that a thing is known. This has been the teachings of the sages of India from the ancient rishis to the 20th century sage of South India, Ramana Maharshi."

He gazed back over the hills, now almost engulfed in the mists. "I don't know whether anyone has actually succeeded in reading my book from cover to cover, and I don't expect people nowadays to understand it. Then why did I write it? Sometimes I muse that there may come a time, an age, when as a species we have evolved such that the understanding I wrestled from the deep is reflected in the common understanding of the day. Maybe they'll marvel, and they will look back in time and say, 'Somebody understood, even back then!' "Maybe I even wrote it for that person in the distant future, just so they know that someone way-back-when saw beyond the horizon of their present day and understood a grain of the truth! It would be like finding a manuscript written in the Middle Ages that demonstrates how the earth revolves around the sun, and that the sun is a rather ordinary star imbedded in one out of a million million galaxies!"

He made a gesture, an upturned palm, that made light of everything. "More probably my book will lie in eternal obscurity." A smile crossed his face. Then he laughed, his white teeth gleaming in the gathering storm.

I took my leave and ran out to where the cows were tethered, distributed the pea shuckings, and ran back inside just as the storm overtook the village.

IV

That night I spent more time with his book, enough to get the gist of it. His ideas were structured on those four forces the physicists have reduced the universe to. He then sees these four forces reflected in everything, from the stages of the individual's life to the four stages of recurring, cyclical human history.

He was not being overly humble when he said the book was not well written. It seemed to be the product of someone whose ideas were secure, but whose writing was hobbled by a certain inability—probably due to a lack of writing experience. Though not necessarily diminishing the validity of his ideas, it did make it difficult to penetrate. He quoted widely and appeared quite well read, especially in Western philosophy and science. This was because he thought the Western, post-Enlightenment scientific gaze was the latest stage in humanity's evolution and he was concerned with what comes next. Many of the authors he referred to were almost quaintly old fashioned, yet solid. He wove together everything from Neils Bohr's interpretation of quantum physics to

Bertrand Russell. He quoted Emerson, Einstein, Sartre, Camus, Galileo, as well as Buddha and especially Lao Tzu. Although he had full command of the English language and possessed a rich vocabulary, his ideas were somehow veiled by the book itself and by the density of his prose, as if in acknowledgement that words could ultimately express what he had to say no more than science could contain it.

His scholarship was messy in places. This bothered me at first. It made me question the whole thing, his theory of the four forces.

I had to wonder whether the force the physicists speak of when they use the word gravity was really the force behind the first of four stages of life, childhood, when the child learns to overcome gravity by learning to stand and to walk.

Was he speaking only metaphorically when he wrote that when the child becomes a youth and enters adolescence, he falls under the sway of the second force, the electro-magnetic force, with its attractions and repulsions, represented by an adolescent's sexual desires, accompanied by love and its opposite, hate?

Could the third force, the strong nuclear force, that which holds the subatomic particles in the atom's nucleus, *really* be the force behind adulthood, of reasoned thought and the founding of a home and family on this earth?

Or the fourth force, what the physicists call the weak nuclear force—responsible for nuclear decay: does he mean to say it is *literally* the force that moves us as individuals or as a culture as a whole beyond the realm of reason, where the dominance of rational thought is replaced by intuition and intimations of the return to what he calls the One, the matrix from which we all derive our being?

Despite its flaws and my natural aversion to all such Theories of Everything, despite the difficulty with which he presented his material, I was beginning to be intrigued—perhaps less about the particulars of his ideas than about the man himself. Who was this man who moved in downstairs, and what had I to do with him? Was he a crank? A sage? Something in-between? Maybe an idiosyncratic mix of the two? He was unquestionably sincere and passionate about his ideas.

In one particularly lucid section he explained that his was a mystic vision, encompassing not only the portion of the cycle that lies between birth and death, when we find ourselves 'entangled' in the forces of nature (Vikram's four forces), and subject to a certain finite span of time; his ideas considered what he called the 'greater circle,' starting with that from which we came and that to which we shall return, a state of uninterrupted oneness, a non-dual state, such as is found at the core of many a mystical school, from Plato on down, and which he insisted is ever present and can be experienced now.

Whether you believe in such a 'greater circle' or not is not important. What is important, in order to understand Vikram's ideas, is that from his point of view, since we are ultimately to become free from these forces, they are not permanently with us; we find ourselves entangled in them, and one by one we can disentangle ourselves from them and be free.

Each stage in life is under one of the forces and presents its lessons to learn, or as he said on many occasions, one must find one's center of balance in the force in order to master it; once you do that you will naturally outgrow that force, that stage in life, that particular stage in the big sweep from the One back to the One. By nature, once you find your balance and come to your center in one of the forces you will then automatically start coming under the influence of the next force, which will present new challenges, throw you off center, and force you to master it. Thus, the boy becomes a youth; the old man learns to grapple with the larger questions as he approaches his end in time.

His was a vision of nature without a creator, arising from the very nature and fabric of the universe itself. If there is One, he contends, then there must be many. They arise together. Just as you cannot talk of light if there was no darkness to juxtapose it. Each force engenders the spontaneous arising of its counter-force, every concept its opposite. It is like a ripple on a still pool: if there is a wave, there must also be a trough. How can you have high without low, big without small, birth without death, or even happy without sad? It would be meaningless for one to exist without the other. Within the One is the very seed of the many; within unity is the seed of division—and vice versa. If you have contraction, you must also have expansion. The mighty oak tree gets contracted into an acorn. The acorn expands into a tree.

Although his ideas were intriguing, I had to wonder just how literally or metaphorically he really took his equating these forces of physics with the development of the individual human being and historical culture. Did he *really* mean to say history has been cycling through these four forces since time immemorial? Were they merely analogous to the forces the physicists speak of? Being something of a scholar myself, and being married to one, there was a lot for me to swallow.

But then I changed tacks. I started looking upon his book as allegory, as if it were an alchemical treatise. Regardless of whether, ultimately, he was writing metaphorically or not, I took it as such. After all, was the philosopher's stone *really* just a stone? Was the gold the alchemists sought really the one found on the chemists' periodic table, something you could take to the jeweler to be tested, weighed, and sold?

He sometimes used facts like a painter used colors: he would mix them in the pallet of his mind, the one influencing the other as profoundly as blue and yellow combine to produce a new color, green, according to some internal, inherent law. One had the impression that since what he wanted to express was beyond words anyway, he had no problem using words and facts in whatever way he deemed necessary to convey what was inherently inexpressible. In this way he was a bit of a trickster, a chameleon, always changing colors, sometimes using contradiction to get his point across, impossible to pin down.

He insisted one should live such that no adjective can stick to you, so no word could pin you down and define you. His scruples were different than that of a scholar. A scholar forms his or her ideas around the facts. Vikram used facts to clothe his ideas. His book, dense as a gnarled block of oak, made an impassioned case for another way of knowing, one that the rational mind had to be almost tricked into not derailing.

I couldn't help being moved by the audacity of what his book attempted to do: it bit off not only a chunk, but the entire universe and offered a unified vision. He had obviously had some profound and shattering experience, what could even be called a *mystical* experience, a vision of wholeness, which his book was written—imperfectly by his own admission—to express.

The first question would naturally be whether his vision was true, whether it offered some fundamental insight, reaching to some sort of ultimate understanding, or whether it was simply the impassioned expression of a man perhaps gone a bit mad by his own inward gaze.

This raises one of the thorniest questions regarding the pronouncements of people who proclaim mystic knowledge. While scientific knowledge is based on rational and repeatable fact, mystic knowledge is based, fundamentally, on individual experience. For a scientific fact to hold true, it must adhere strictly to cause and effect. If the conditions of a particular experiment are met, if the causes are the same, then the results must be reproducible for a scientific truth to be arrived at, whether the experiment is conducted in New York or Tokyo. Mystic experience, by contrast, is by its very nature individual and unique, idiosyncratic, and particular. Perhaps there are no conditions that must be met to produce mystic experience.

Regardless of whether you have ever experienced a mystical insight, whether you believe they exist or whether you think they are a load of bunk and that everyone who has ever claimed one is subject to delusion, one must at least acknowledge that in most every time and clime, in cultures from East to West, from the Old World to the New, from Europe to Africa, from India to Central America, from the 21st century stretching back at least to the dawn of history, there have always been people who have claimed to have had fundamental mystical experience. In fact, many great movements of human culture have been founded by such people, including most of the world's major religions.

Those who have studied such things have found certain common elements in the mystics' insights, such as a powerful experience of oneness. They speak of a certain level of seeing, a way of perceiving the world, that comes upon one in an instant, and which lays bare the unity behind diversity, a unifying, binding, and sometimes blindingly powerful force that some have called Love, some God, some Tao, some Buddha Nature. Some simply use the word Truth with a capital T.

Again, whether you believe their experiences are true or not, it is an experience purported from most every time, place, and culture. It is an element of the human condition, a human phenomenon, and therefore, I believe, worthy of examination.

Another common element to the mystics' path is that it often comes at a cost. The mystic must die to who and what they were, as if a new body and mind, a new vessel were needed to contain their insight. It is even said mystics are the 'twice-born,' those who have died while living. It involves a transformation, practically a new birth, perhaps what the caterpillar experiences when it emerges as a butterfly.

The literature is full of people driven to the point of despair, who experience the dissolution of the ego, surrender to something greater, a sort of death and rebirth, often wrestling with the deepest and darkest forces in places most of us would not go—not unless compelled. Think of Jesus in the desert tempted by Satan; Buddha under the Bodhi tree and his encounter with the demon Mara. There are innumerable other mystics, less well known or even entirely obscure, people who base their knowing not on anything learned or what can be taught, but who have undergone similar transformative experiences. They have what they call their direct experience and base their knowing on that, which of course flies in the face of the thinking of our rational age.

Because they have experience, they tend to act as if they know, as if their knowing is unassailable. And it is true, on a certain level, that to truly know something is to have experienced it. Hearing about the sweetness of honey is not the same as tasting it. There is a different level of knowing. While you might be able to use words to describe the taste of honey from what you've read or from what others have told you, he who has tasted honey, while he might not be able to express it, he alone will know it. That is how mystics tend to speak, how they write, how they express what they've experienced.

And just because someone has had experience of what the mystics speak, it doesn't mean he or she has either the wish or the capability to express it. The experience can come through anyone, literate or illiterate, high born or low; one time it could be a poet-philosopher, the next a carpenter. It could even be some-one who to all the world appears an idiot. Yet they redefine what the human organism is capable of, what understanding is possible, often sputtering near unintelligible words of oneness, of love, of unity, sometimes imagined as a land beyond cares, what some describe as a place of bliss.

Some say we all knew this state in childhood and that we can see it reflected in a baby's face. Plato says all true learning is but a remembering of what we knew before the trauma of our birth as separate beings. Wordsworth wrote his poem about the child's intimations of immortality, saying babies and young children still know the paradise we are searching for, before it 'fades into the light of common day.' This is what Vikram would call the oneness from which we come and to which we ultimately shall all return, which, because it is unitary, arises concurrently with its very opposite, the manifest world and all the separate things and creatures that inhabit it.

The way to this understanding is not easy. It is not likely many will undertake such a journey. For instance, I am myself probably too comfortable in my skin and with my life to burn it all away. Usually, if you look at the life story of a mystic, you will find something that compelled them to go so far. Often it is pain, some maladjustment of their selves with the world, something that forces them to dive in such deep and dangerous waters.

Mystics are rare. Their paths are by definition idiosyncratic by the very fact that they have passed through, overcome, or simply disregarded what the existing social and societal world expects of them. They dive deep into the borderlands of human experience, deep into the ocean of being, and come back with a vision, a notion, an insight, or a boon. Mystics are varied and individual. They have plowed their row so deep that they hit some sort of gold. Some go mad in the process. Some are certainly cranks, people with an oversized opinion of their place in the world.

V

The next morning I met Vikram again on the back veranda. My interest had been piqued, and though the compost bucket was only half filled, I took it out, hoping he would be there. I felt something was perhaps happening. We had lived in this house for good chunks of the year for the past twelve years. I had been despairing a little of late—wondering when, where, and even *whether* the next story would come. I had told myself many times that for a story to be yours, it will have to come naturally. You cannot go out looking for it. Nothing had come for quite a long time. I had recently been wondering whether it ever would. There was no guarantee. There was nothing I could do.

When I opened the door to cross the back veranda he was there again, pacing back and forth with his hands clasped behind his back, his steps deliberate. He smiled when he saw me and stopped.

He began talking. Again, I had the feeling he had been thinking of what to say. This time he wanted to speak not so much about his ideas, but about his life, and he started at the very beginning, with his birth. I didn't quite know why he wanted to tell me all this, but he was determined. It seemed he was a man of tremendous will, and was used to exerting it. It almost felt as if I were being ambushed.

"I was marked from birth," he began, "stamped you could almost say, labeled with an adjective with which I've had to wrestle my entire life. You see, quite literally from the moment I was born there was the expectation put upon me that I would become some kind of holy man, an enlightened saint, what we in India call a baba. It was all because of this," and he pushed the loose sleeve of his cotton kurta to his elbow. Extending his arm, he showed me the underside of his forearm, which was dominated by a long, oblong-shaped thick black birthmark with straight white hairs growing out of it.

"This birthmark was identical to the birthmark on a saint's arm who had recently expired at a very advanced age. Naturally—if you know anything of Indian culture—they thought I was him, the ancient sage come back into the body of a child.

Just imagine what this was like, being raised as if I had special mystic knowledge. My mother even consulted me as an oracle. But, being an intelligent boy, I had to ask *myself*, especially as I grew older, whether I really had that direct connection with the god, the force, or whatever mystic knowledge they thought it was that I possessed. So you see, even as a boy, I had to ask the deeper questions. It was imposed upon me along with this birthmark on my arm. It forced me to ask the deeper questions from an unnaturally early age. Such was the force of the label that was placed upon me."

Vikram got a glint in his eye, mischievous, as if he was imparting a secret. He lowered his voice: "Live such that no one can make an adjective stick to you. That's what it taught me. Accept no one's label. In fact, confuse them. Act one way one moment, and another way the next. Make them wonder. Make them guess. Is he a good man or a bad? Could he really be a saint? Or is he a rogue? What is he? Is he a mystic, or is he just a fool?

"Yes, let nothing stick to you, and be stuck to nothing. Then you will be free—free to be spontaneous, free to be who and what you originally are, free to act on the great stage without undue identification with whatever role the moment calls upon you to play. That is the real freedom. It has nothing to do with the chains another man can put you in. It is the chains you put yourself that are the most difficult to loosen. They are invisible and often unconscious.

"If they can define you, if society can make a label stick, if they think they know who or what you are, then, quite naturally, and perhaps unconsciously, you will begin conforming to that expectation. You'll start fitting into their box. In one stroke, you will have lost both your freedom and your spontaneity. Yes, better to be a shape-shifter and keep them guessing. If even one adjective sticks to you then you are not traveling as light as you can, and you cannot pass through."

I cannot now remember precisely how we came to the idea that I would hear and perhaps write his story. But it happened that day, as I stood there with the compost bucket half-filled on the back veranda. Maybe I don't remember how we decided because it already seemed a foregone conclusion, the logical outcome of his living downstairs and me upstairs. It was as if we both knew that's what it was all about. It was a natural match, a writer looking for a story and a man with one to tell.

All I know is that by the end of our encounter that day on the veranda we had agreed that I would come down the next morning

at ten o'clock, and that we would take up his story in a more serious and consistent way.

And so it was that during that entire rainy season I came down
for one and often two sessions a day. We sat in his front room on
two old wooden chairs separated by a small round wooden table,
his windows open wide to the intermittent and sometimes heavy
monsoon rain. When the clouds came low, or rose up from the valley and the fog entered the room we were literally steeped in it.
Monsoon in India, especially in the rural mountainous areas, is
a peaceful and languorous time of year. People don't travel. It is
too wet to work the fields, too wet to go about. That's what added
to the remarkable situation: even though it was the monsoon, I
didn't need an umbrella or mud boots to go to him! I'd just kick on
my chappals, gather up my paper and pen, and, often balancing a
hot cup of coffee, go downstairs to the back veranda.

Knocking gently on his screen door I'd let myself in. Usually,
he would already be sitting in his front room and with a gesture
invite me to sit. And without chitchat about the weather, unless
it had been extreme, he'd clear his throat and just start speaking.

It always seemed obvious that he had been thinking about
what to say, even though he often picked up far from where he
left off the day before. Early on, I tried to keep him on track and
ask him such innocent questions as, "And then what happened?"
But because of his hearing, normal conversation was not possible. If I interrupted him, as I often tried to early on, he either
wouldn't notice or he would stop his monologue to listen and lip-
read and guess my meaning, but it was often a struggle.

We had these strange and often useless conversations, like
when I interrupted him to ask his age at a particular point in his
story.

"What was your age?" I asked.

"What page?" He cupped his hand around his ear to better
hear.

"No. *Age.* What *age* were you?"

"What was my name?"

And on and on. So whenever I had a question or comment that
was important enough to merit an interruption, I would hold my
hand out to signal him to stop, tear a page out of my notebook,

and write the question out. Then I'd hold it up to him. He would put on his reading glasses and read it, then answer—or not, according to his fancy.

The entire process of stopping him, writing out my question, then showing it to him broke his flow to such an extent that I interrupted him only when absolutely necessary. He was well able to speak without a break for an hour or two at a time, and to continue unabated until I had to stop him to tell him I had to go to lunch or whatever it was I had to do.

He was a great and enthusiastic story teller, gesticulating the whole time, often breaking off into laughter, in turns serious and treating it as if it were all nothing, of no importance whatsoever. His hands were seldom at rest. This was all in such contrast to his written word, where his words tended to veil and obscure his ideas, probably because the written word has pretenses to permanency. He once said that this entire life, it comes and goes, and that we should not give in to the illusion of permanence. All of life, he said, is like writing on water.

And what was even more remarkable was that though he read English books, even the English poets and philosophers, and even though he wrote in English, he had only rarely had the opportunity to actually *speak* it. English for him was like a scholar's Latin, read, but rarely heard. His vocabulary was superb, and he was well capable of expressing difficult ideas and all the emotions of his tumultuous life.

His accent, however, was difficult. He tended to add a syllable at the end of his words, often with a vowel sound, much like Italians sometimes do when speaking English. So it took quite some getting used to, and a lot of concentration.

Since he directed the flow of the narrative with minimal intervention on my part, the ordering of his story was almost as individual and idiosyncratic as he was. He picked up and dropped themes and phases of his life in what could only be termed an organic manner, the hidden threads of narrative known only to himself. It sometimes left my head spinning. Since it was so difficult to interrupt, I gave in. I listened attentively, took notes, and trusted that in the end I'd have a record of the whole story from beginning to end and from top to bottom. What else could I do?

Although we were engaged in a project with a common purpose, namely his imparting to me the stories that made up his life, we had different reasons for spending the monsoon doing so. I was interested in perhaps one day writing his story, even though from the start we were clear that although we were both expending an extraordinary amount of time and energy, I was under no obligation to do so. From his side I often had the feeling that by telling his tale, by laying it out in all its details as he had never done before, he was in some way coming to terms with the strange and sometimes unsettling course his life had taken, that it somehow fit in his own evolution, that in the telling there was also a reckoning. It sometimes seemed I was recording his confession.

In the pages that follow I have worked Vikram's story into a coherent whole, occasionally filling in the gaps. Given my preference for true stories of real people, you might well ask whether what follows is fiction or non-fiction. The most accurate and honest answer would be that though the stories are his, the words, while retaining his voice, are mine. I have shaped his story, and tell it mostly upon the chronological ordering of events. In other words, beginning at the beginning.

Now that the context has been provided for the story that follows, I will retreat to the background and let Vikram tell the story himself, just as he spoke it to me, that is, without interruption. Therefore, I hand it over to him, and I will return in the Epilogue.

CHAPTER 2

VIKRAM BEGINS HIS STORY FROM BEFORE THE BEGINNING

You might think for me to tell the story of my life it would be best to start at the beginning. While this would generally be true, in my case we'll have to start before the beginning. For the first twelve years of their marriage, my parents had only daughters, three daughters, and one stillborn son. If you know anything of Indian culture, especially in our Punjab, and especially at that time, in the 1940s, you can imagine that this was a problem.

While Guru Nanak, our Sikh religions' founder, taught the equality of women, sons were still important. In our culture, while daughters get married and become part of their husband's family, a son brings a wife into the family and stays to take over the land, house, and business if they have one as his parents age. A son, especially in those days, was as necessary as a pension is today. Without a son, who will take care of you in your old age? Because the Punjab has been fighting the whole of its history and only men fought, having sons was especially important in our Punjab. It was felt that a son in the family must be there, also to carry on the family's legacy. This is how it was in those days, and it is somewhat true today.

My father was quite liberal and ahead of the times. He loved his daughters and didn't bother much about having a son. But my mother very much wanted to give birth to a son. She may have felt pressure from others in the family, perhaps from her mother-in-law. I do not know, since I was obviously not there.

Anyway, after twelve years and three daughters, a religious procession was crossing through our village and passed in front of our house. It was celebrating the birth anniversary of one of the Sikh's ten gurus.

My mother was pregnant and ready to give birth. She had thought it auspicious to give birth on this special day commemorating a saint's birth. Just as the procession was passing the house, my mother gave birth—to another stillborn son.

Somebody told my father, who was in the procession. The procession stopped. People began to sympathize and to lament with my father and the rest of the family. Then someone called out, "Let us pray to God that before the next anniversary a son comes to this house!" So they prayed a son would come.

It went something like that. That was the story the people of my village—my neighbors, my sisters, and especially my mother—told me as far back as I can remember.

What happened then was that my *masi*—that's what we call a maternal aunt in Punjabi, my mother's sister—suggested, it must have been some days or a month or so later, that though prayer was OK, they should go to a neighboring village where she heard that a local holy man, a saint, happened to be residing for a time. Saints in those days used to travel from village to village. He was a travelling baba, quite famous throughout the region. People believed he could give boons. I could show you his photo. If you want, you can come with me to the Punjab and I'll show you his shrine. I could show you the cave where he used to meditate.

So together with my auntie and my three older sisters, my mother walked to this neighboring village to ask this saint for his blessings so she could give birth to a living son.

The saint, clad in a white robe, was sitting cross-legged on a blanket under a huge sprawling tree. He was ancient, looking ready to pass over into the next world at any time. At a respectful distance sat a small group of people, a few of his closest disciples and some local villagers. They indicated that the little group around my mother should sit directly before him.

Everyone's attention was drawn to the saint. His eyes were closed. He was in a deep state of absorption, what we call *samadhi*. Saints in those days were not like the saints of today, who are quite money-minded. They would enter a state of absorption, go into themselves, become one with the One—whatever you want to call it. Back then they didn't care who came and went. They had and needed nothing. They would beg for their daily food.

So he was sitting like that. After some time he opened his eyes and looked at my mother, her sister, and her three young daughters. He looked at the youngest and said, "What is your name, little boy?" With babies, you sometimes can't tell the difference.

There ensued an embarrassed silence, which my auntie broke: "This is not a boy," she said, her eyes lowered. "She is a girl. We have come for my sister here. She has had only daughters, and we've come to ask for your blessing so she can have a son."

My mother was shy about asking the saint for a son; so she was glad that her sister, whose idea it was in the first place, had broached the subject for her.

The saint went back into silence. His eyes closed. After a time, he came to again. There was a bowl of fruits and other offerings before him. He reached in and gave my mother two small yellow fruits with the words, "May God fulfill your wish," or something like that.

He became silent again. Maybe he was reciting the name of God, or remembering God, or whatever it is they used to do. I don't know. And when he came to, he asked them which village they were from. They told him.

He was silent a few moments, his eyes trained on my mother, then he slowly spoke. "I will be coming to your village," he said. And with that the interview was over and my mother, auntie, and sisters got up and walked back to our village.

I cannot know exactly what really happened. But this is the story I heard over and again from my mother, my auntie, and my sisters, especially my oldest sister, who was old enough at the time to remember.

When he said he'd be coming to our village, my mother thought he was actually saying, "I'm coming to you! I will not only come *to* you, but I will come *through* you, I will take birth through you." Maybe she imagined it, but this is the way she heard it. She never had a doubt. He was so old and so near death that she thought what he really meant was that he would incarnate in her village and take birth through her.

She is the only one who heard it that way. Everyone else thought he meant he'd next be coming to their village. Remember, he was a traveling baba. This majority interpretation seemed borne out a few days later when he in fact came to their village riding atop a tall horse colorfully decked out, with his attendants following on foot. They stopped at the village Gurudwara, our Sikh temple, and tethered the horse. It was there he would hold court and spend the night.

At about two in the morning, the attendants heard a commotion. The horse was prancing around and neighing, stamping his hoofs on the ground, clearly spooked by something.

One of the attendants went to check on the saint—and the saint was dead!

Chapter 3

Taking Birth

It was about ten months later—nine months, maybe ten months or so, maybe in the same year—that I took birth from my mother. And I was alive and kicking, hale and hardy.

As I told you, the saint had had a birthmark on the underside of his forearm, about four inches long. It was jet-black and he was known for it. He was even nicknamed after it.

When I was born with the same birthmark and my mother saw it, she was convinced of what she'd heard the saint say, that he'd be taking incarnation through her. My auntie, my sisters, everybody was instantly convinced. And when the main disciple of that dead saint saw my birthmark, he began to weep. "My guru has been reborn—he has come back. He has not left me. My guru has taken reincarnation!"

Just imagine—from before I can remember they thought I was a saint, a baba, a god-man! My mother never had a doubt, right to her dying day. She thought whatever I said would come to pass, that I could predict the future.

It was only much later that she started calling me a saint gone bad, a misfit saint!

She said this because once I left home I did just the opposite of what a saint was supposed to do. I went to the other side, to the other extreme. But that comes later.

The important thing to note here is that from the earliest age the persona of a saint was imposed on me.

And that's not all, it wasn't only that I was supposed to be a saint. My mother was very protective of me, especially when I was very young. She didn't like me playing with the other kids if she wasn't watching. "Don't go out. Don't

27

go there, don't go out of my sight. Somebody will take you; they'll snatch you and take you away forever. They might even kill you!"

This is how it was in the villages in those days: let us say some other woman can't get a child. It sometimes happens that this woman without a child comes to believe that her child, the child destined for her, gets born to another woman, and that this other woman, who became pregnant and gave birth to what was supposed to be *her* child, had maneuvered things, gotten some magic from somebody, in order to snatch this baby's soul.

There were some relatives of my mother, some sort of distant cousins, a couple who found themselves unable to have children. My mother was convinced—I suppose this woman had said something to my mother, she had apparently confronted my mother shortly after my birth—that my mother had snatched my soul on the way down and though I was supposed to be born to this relative, took my soul through magical means and gave birth to me herself! Such was the level of belief in those days.

My mother was convinced that this woman would try to do me harm, maybe by giving me poison, some mercury or something like that, to kill me in revenge. She had openly accused my mother of taking away her son.

This is why my mother was afraid. I was special because of my birthmark—and for being at risk of kidnap and death. I remember this especially when I was a preschooler. She kept a close eye on me and wouldn't let me play with the other kids. So at the same tender age that she was instilling in me that I had special saintly powers and could be questioned like an oracle, there was also the fear that I might be snatched away, that someone may harm me, that someone might take me from my mother. By the time I went to school, my mother had relaxed. I think this other woman had her own child and forgot that I was hers. What persisted was the saint thing.

When I was a small child that baba's main disciple would come through our village, stopping at various houses to collect his daily food. When he came to our house, they'd fetch me. He would bow down before me and put his forehead to my birthmark.

Sometimes he would begin crying: "My master, my guru, my *sat guru*!" Things like that.

He came almost daily. Sometimes I wasn't home, maybe I was playing somewhere or, when older, I might already have left for school. Some days he may have been in a hurry. But most days he would come to our house especially to see me. Often he carried his *khunda*, his ritual staff, a gift from the saint as a mark of his discipleship, with gold and jewels fixed on it. He would rest it on the crown of my head to charge it.

I laugh now, but at the time I was quite serious, and seriously confused as to whether I really was something special, whether I had a special relationship with God—however my young self might have conceived it.

It doesn't matter whether I was the saint's reincarnation. It matters less what your views are on reincarnation, and whether there is such a thing. It doesn't matter whether my birthmark was a miracle or something that can be easily explained by your Western science. None of that matters: the reality is that from before I can remember, this mark on my arm meant that the whole saint thing was imposed upon me.

Even up until the time I was old enough for school I was really enjoying it. Always getting special attention, being singled out. Sometimes people brought me extra sweets! And it became even more enjoyable later, during my young school days, when I started going along with it, when I began to *play* the role of the baba! My audience was mainly my mother, my sisters, and all my aunties. I had a ball!

I didn't know anything, but I had seen photos of that saint. I knew how saints would sit. Since they sat cross-legged, straight-backed, with eyes half closed, I thought I must also sit like this. I acted as if there was some god or some kind of force that I was in touch with, especially when my mother was nearby. I'd roll my eyes up in their sockets and sit perfectly still.

I would go to the Gurudwara, our village temple. Usually it was empty, but sometimes I'd see the old babas there reciting the holy books. I watched how they would sit in silence remembering God—or whatever it was that they were doing. Sometimes they were reading and discussing the scriptures amongst themselves or with their disciples. They also performed rituals.

I was an intelligent child, and watched carefully and learned how babas acted. Soon I realized I could attract more attention if I sat with a holy book and appeared to be studying it. In those days, everybody was religious and had the holy books in their house. So I would take a book from the family shrine and I would sit before one of those low wooden tables. I would place a cloth on it. Then I'd place the holy book on that, sit cross-legged on a pillow behind it, and pretend to read.

Of course, being so young, I could make out nothing of what was in those books and gained nothing from them. I had only just learned to read. I let my finger run slowly along the lines as if I were reading. Then I would look off into empty space as if in deep contemplation. I repeated things that were written, having no idea what any of it meant. How could I? I was only a child.

To say I was pretending would miss the complexity of my situation. For while I was putting it on, while I was acting in such a way as to gain attention and to fulfil that expectation laid upon me at birth, at the same time I was asking myself whether I really was a baba.

My mother was already convinced that whatever I said would come true. Imagine what that is like for a little boy! I half believed it myself. How couldn't I, with my mother and the neighbors, especially the women, and even more so the disciple of that saint all making me out to be a saint? They all sort of made me one; they put into my head that I was somebody special. So who was I to dispute it?

This was the pressure from the outside; but from within the pressure was even more intense when I started asking *myself* whether I really had special abilities, and couldn't find them. So there was this furious storm going on in my head.

The only one who didn't like all this talk about babas was my father. Though he was a religious man—everybody was in those days—he did not believe in all these itinerant babas and what he saw as their tricks. He thought most of them were fakes. He believed only in the holy book, the Guru Granth Sahib, the holy book of the Sikhs—only that.

When they first went to the neighboring village for the saint's blessing, back before I was born, my mother and auntie had tried to get my father to come along; but my father had refused. Then he had forbidden them to go. He was very strict. In the end, they had snuck there without his knowledge.

So as I was growing up, the entire baba thing had to be hidden from my father. His work was some five kilometers from our village. He would leave in the morning and come back only at night. While he was gone, when I wasn't playing with my friends, I would be playing the baba. But by the time my father came home, the low table and the books, everything, would be cleaned up and nobody would say a word. When my father was home I became once again just a little boy.

So that persona of a saint, it sat on my head. I began to think I may be—I must be—a saint. I *must* be somebody. Am I a saint? Do I have special powers? How do I reach them? At the time, I hardly separated my playacting the role of a saint from my questioning whether I really was one. In my childish mind I thought I must be a saint if everybody says I am—how could it be otherwise?—yet I didn't feel like one. Where were my special powers?

This is how I spent my boyhood.

One other thing that happened to me as a boy had a tremendous effect on my entire life. It happened when I was five or six years old. I got a high fever. I suppose I wasn't taken to a doctor in time, or there were none in rural post-Partition Punjab, but the outcome was that I lost my hearing to the extent that it is gone today. I can hear a little bit, especially certain frequencies, but not much, as I'm sure you have noticed.

I actually think going deaf was a great blessing. I have always had too much energy. The life force in me has always been in full flush. It's been like this my entire life. If my hearing had been intact and I had been able to fully engage with the world I would have gotten lost in it. With the kind of energy I've had, I could have earned a lot of money and built up property and position. As they say, I would have gained the world and lost my soul. Since my hearing prevented me from going too far outside, I had no choice but to go within. My loss of hearing prevented me from going too badly astray.

Now I am this old man. And in the end, I have no power or position in this world. Nothing. Yet I've seen the beauty with which life unfolds. I've seen some horror too. It is the greatest journey to explore the life within.

CHAPTER 4

STIRRINGS FROM BELOW

We shifted villages when I was about ten years old. So we left the village where the saint had died and where I was born. My sisters were of the age to start their higher secondary education, and there was no school close to our village that admitted girls. My father, being quite ahead of his time, believed girls should receive an education. So we moved, and in the new village nobody knew about the saint that died or the significance of my birthmark. The disciples of that saint never came there.

With nobody in the village knowing about it and my father's opposition to the whole thing, my being a baba was now confined to a very small circle, mainly my mother and sisters and my auntie when she would visit. For them, it was still the same, and I was treated almost with deference. But for the rest of the world I was just another child. And I wondered—the question persisted: Am I a saint, a baba? Do I have powers? Do I have a special connection with the god?

When I came to my thirteenth or fourteenth year, some new and unforeseen force began to stir within me: I began to be attracted to girls. That this happens to boys of that age, I didn't know. Or I didn't know it would happen to me! It came as a total surprise. And remember, I could hardly hear, so I could not hear the jokes of the other boys.

My conception of how to be a saint or a god-man was rather conventional: it was by being a good boy, by living a pure and pious life. I was yet to know that the Hindu god Ram had killed, that Moses was a murderer, or that the great poet saint of Tibet, Milarepa, had murdered many. I didn't know that one must muddy oneself in this world, that one must lose one's innocence through experience, that angels are not enough. You need your demons too, and you must fight with them. I knew none of that. So I was actually struggling against the tide—against the very flow of life coursing through my bloodstream in the form of hormones—by trying to remain pure.

Once this libidinal force began brewing, it quickly took me over: it was like a hurricane, like a flood, like a dam that had burst. It was beyond my control. My saint persona had been kept very much alive, if almost in secret, by my mother, my sisters, and my auntie. Now this persona ran into direct conflict with nature.

Thoughts came quite spontaneously to my mind—as they will to a boy of that age. I got the urge to—to do something, perhaps. As a child does, he touches this, that. I also wanted to do what every young man of that age does. You can understand that. You must also have done the same.

And so I also started doing this thing. Sexual desire took over my thinking. On the one hand, I had these new urges raging inside me. My hands would go there. "Don't" my mind would say. "Saints don't look at girls. Saints don't do *that!*"

I had a photo of the saint that died. In fact it was taken just after he completed. That's what we in the Punjab say when someone dies. We say *poora hogia,* he has completed. It was his death photo, and I used to look at his closed eyes, his sunken cheeks, and ask myself with a chill running up my spine whether I could really be him. Surely, during his whole long life of being a saint he had controlled his desires. He didn't do anything like *that!* Surely, he remained in *samadhi,* absorbed in the name of God, or whatever it was that saints did.

Not knowing whether I really had special powers, I remember wishing for some sort of assurance, some proof from God that he was there. If only I knew I had a special connection, then I would have had *double* the strength with which to resist. I would have had some reason not to do it, and I would be able to control myself. Then I could say to God, with whom I would have a direct line of communication, "Give me the power to resist. Give me that power for whatever purpose you have in store for me; whatever you want me to do with this power, just let me know what it is.

But first you must give me proof." Even if it didn't relieve my tensions, at least I would have had the blessing of God—or whatever force—and I could have controlled myself.

My thinking ran like this: if I am really a saint or something, then I must not do it. But if not, if I have no special connection, then to hell with it! Leave me alone. Let me start living like other kids. Let me start *enjoying* my life!

No one knew of my inner conflict. How could they? It was all silent talk within myself. What was I to do? I had to find out whether I was some kind of saint! But who could I ask?

My mother told me that God exists, but she could never show me any proof. None of them could—and especially not that I had some special link. People spoke of God, and when I asked them about it, it was clear, even though I was but a child, that they were only talking. It was only words. No one knew what they were talking about. Nobody had actually seen or heard from him.

My mother told me, "Go daily to the temple, bow low before the altar, read the holy scriptures, don't tell any lie, and especially don't look at any girl—and then you will be able to see God."

The village temple was close to our house. It was a small one with an upstairs room where no one ever went. Before school I would go there, also after school, and in my spare time and on holidays. My mother had told me that to find God I should read the Gutka, one of the scriptures of our Sikh religion. Like everyone, we had a copy in the house, so I would bring it there to the upstairs room of the temple. Or sometimes I would go to some other isolated place. My mother told me I should read it from front to back a certain number of times, maybe twelve, maybe a hundred—I cannot now recall. She told me that is how saints found God. So I did it. I read this book the prescribed number of times from front to finish, of course not comprehending a thing.

The Gutka begins with these lines, the first words that our founder, Guru Nanak, uttered after he reached enlightenment. It is called the Mool Mantar, the Root Verse. It begins with *Ik Onkaar*, God is one, the source of everything. *Satnaam*, his name is Truth. *Kartaa Purkh*, he is the doer. This is how the book begins.

So without understanding anything of what I was reading, I read, and when finished reading, I read it again, and again, and again—never understanding what was written inside it. I just knew I had to read the holy book and God will appear.

I cannot now recall how many days or months passed like this, my sneaking off in every spare moment to read through this book. Probably two or three months.

When I closed the book after reading it that prescribed number of times I thought now and for sure God will appear before me and tell me what it is he wants with me. There was even a little break in the clouds and sunbeams were streaming in through the open window. I thought I would hear God's voice, perhaps in a blinding light, "Here I am, my boy!"

But nothing happened.

Not only were my hormones flowing at full flood, but my thirst for the proof of God was raging—I really wanted to see God. Actually, I wanted to have it out with him. I wanted to *confront* him! Maybe not confront him, but I wanted to see him. I wanted to ask him: Have I really any special connection with you?

One day, I was alone upstairs in the temple. It was the only place I was ever alone. In India, you're never alone. I was in such a heightened state of tension, my saintly thoughts vying for supremacy with those of a more carnal nature, that I thought I would burst. My hands wanted to do one thing to relieve a certain tension—and in the temple no less!—while my mind wanted them to do something else—to press palms in some sort of supplication before some holy presence.

In desperation and full of passion—such as can only be mustered by a thirteen-year-old—I spoke aloud to God, "If I really have a special connection with you, then appear before me. I want to see you. Show yourself!"

My heart was pounding, my eyes wide open, ready for God to appear in any of his glorious guises—but of course nothing happened.

I made excuses for God. I thought it must be my fault, not his. Could I have told a lie to my parents about some sweets? Could I unknowingly have told a lie to somebody else? Surely, I could have. How would I know? Maybe it was because I had been late for school one morning and hadn't gone to the temple to bow down before the altar. This also may have happened.

Or I might have looked at that girl from my class a few seconds too long.

Then I thought maybe God is not like some human being. Maybe God has his own reasons not to appear before me.

"If you cannot appear before me in person," I bargained, "just show me in some way, in some indirect way, that you are there."

I took a brick and placed it at the corner of the low table upon which I had laid that book.

"OK, God: If you hear me, if we have some special connection, and if for some reason you cannot show yourself, then move this brick from this side of the table to that!"

Needless to say, the brick did not move.

People were always praying to God for rain, or to stop the rain if the nearby Beas River was in flood. So the next time, when I was sure I hadn't lied in the interim, when I hadn't even raised my eye when a girl was walking by—let alone let it linger on her, arousing decidedly unsaintly thoughts—when I had been faithful in my prayers, I made my next demand, which I thought would be easier for God to fulfill: "OK, God. If you are listening, make it rain within the next fifteen minutes!"

Not a drop fell.

So I moderated my demand even further: "Please God, show yourself to me in whatever form *you* like. Just give me a sign, the sign of your choice. Just let me know whether I have some special connection with you." What I really wanted to say was, "Prove it, God damn it!"

CHAPTER 5

LOVE AT FIRST SIGHT

One day, something happened to change everything. I must have been in my fourteenth or fifteenth year. It was summer, the middle of the monsoon, but it was a beautiful sunny day. There was a big fair and celebration happening in a village across the fields. I think it was our Independence Day, which would make it August 15. Your country, America, also has a day celebrating independence from the Brits. Yours I believe is in July. Ours is in August.

Anyway, there was this big function in a neighboring village and my three older sisters wanted to go. I was less keen on going because of my hearing, especially since if my sisters met their friends I wouldn't be able to partake. I was more absorbed with my own things anyway. Even though they were older than me, my father told me to take my sisters to the fair and to bring them home. Girls did not go about in those days to neighboring villages without a male chaperone from the family. Even though still a child, I was old enough now to act as chaperone and protector of the family honor.

When we got there the place was packed. There were stalls and games and hawkers of all the varieties of cheap things that people from backward, rural villages back then bought—buckets and woven baskets, tools for digging and plowing, trinkets and slingshots and toys for the boys and bracelets for the girls.

There was a stage, and when we got there the program had already begun. Punjabi singers wearing some kind of traditional dress were dancing around and singing. Then some politician or important person who had been standing just offstage started delivering a speech. He must have been a special VIP. Everybody stopped what they were doing and concentrated on what he had to say, clapping now and again with great enthusiasm. He was probably speaking about our newly formed democracy and how with independence from the British we must now govern ourselves and set our own destiny. There was much of this patriotic talk in those days.

But since I couldn't hear what he was saying, my attention was drawn elsewhere. This hearing loss I attained when I was five or six has often led me to what is missed by others. In this case, the freedom I achieved by not being attracted by some politician's speech led me to an experience that was to change everything for me. It at once resolved all my problems—and gave me an entire set of new ones!

It is said that Alexander the Great expanded his empire as far east as the Punjab, where some of his soldiers settled and married locals. Thus, Greek blood is occasionally mixed with local blood, usually to quite striking effect.

My eye was ranging over the sea of people when I saw a young girl of my own age standing a short distance away. The moment I saw her I was stunned, thunderstruck by her beauty—but it was more than that. It was as if a princess had stepped out of a book of legend. There was magic in it, as if she came from another world. Perhaps she suddenly got up, or maybe she turned her head at the same instant as I, but when our eyes met something happened.

Love, especially as conceived by a young teenager, would not describe what I felt or experienced. It was rather as if time came to a standstill and I had a glimpse of some greater whole, something outside of time. Her world and my world fused into one, and I *knew* it was the same for her. We were like two waves on a vast ocean falling into sync and becoming one. I didn't know that this could happen. But the moment our eyes met, my life began a new course.

I was no longer alone. The world sparkled. Everything was renewed like after a spring rain. It happened in an instant, and in that instant a new world was revealed. It was as if God had finally shown himself—but not in the form I had expected, not connected to all that goody-goody saintly stuff with some gray-bearded god.

This was with a living girl!

It was love at first sight.

It turned out we lived on opposite ends of the same village. She had just moved there, and we could see each other from our rooftops. Deep down I was still challenging God, questioning him, even reprimanding him: Why didn't you appear to me in person? Now look what a mess I'm in—I'm getting entangled with a girl!

That girl and I would sometimes meet. After school I used to go to a village a kilometer away where there was a field where us boys used to play ball. We all belonged to different villages and would meet there.

One day, when the sun was nearing the horizon and our game was over, I set off walking home. Since I was the only boy from my village that day I was walking alone. She was waiting for me at the edge of the field, and we walked together all the way back to our village. It turned out she was quite forward, even daring. I'm sure she expected, as any girl normally would, that I would do something, talk to her, anything, maybe even try to touch her. We didn't even exchange a word.

Despite this, she came again a few days later. I saw her waiting at the edge of the field. But this time there were other boys from my village and I felt embarrassed. Normally, us boys would walk home together joking and laughing and kicking stones along the way. I pretended I'd forgotten something on the other end of the field and told the boys from my village that I would catch up. So I waited until they were well underway.

Without saying a word, she started walking beside me. It was electrifying just to be near her, like being in a magic, charmed sphere. We didn't even try to exchange a word. I didn't as much as touch her, even though I had this uncontrollable fantasy that she would take me forcibly in her arms and kiss me on the lips!

I was unusually naive and unsophisticated as a boy, innocent of the ways of the world. For one, I could not hear. For another, there were these two powerful forces on a collision course, one driven by testosterone and the other was nurtured by my mother's and sisters' and auntie's insistence that I was not a normal boy, but the incarnation of a realized saint.

I honestly tried to be a good boy, but this girl was always trying to waylay me. She would send me love letters and suggest we meet in some secluded spot. I met her a few times, but never took the initiative to do something or touch her—even though she was waiting and more than willing, daring even. Oh, how much difficulty she put me through! Sometimes she would say something, and though I could not hear, I was sure she was making a mockery of me. We would meet secretly and just stand there in awkward silence, and then return to our homes.

In rural village Punjab, especially in those days, boys and girls didn't go around much with each other. Marriages were arranged and virtually everyone was a virgin before marriage. Some daring ones would meet and touch, maybe just their hands; some really daring ones would kiss; *rarely* would they go beyond that. It was pretty much unheard of—except when there was a resulting pregnancy. This always spelled the ruin of both parties involved and cast a stain of shame upon both families.

Things were also complicated in my case because of caste. A girl who went around with a boy was already thought of as a bad or a loose girl, a stain that often persisted for the rest of her life. To some extent boys could be boys, but the girls' honor was a reflection on the family. If the boy was of a relatively high caste and the girl low, it was even worse for the girl, doubly bad. Since no alliance could ever be sanctified by marriage between such a pair, it would be seen as if she was prostituting herself and she may never find a husband. And this girl was of such a low caste that she could have been our servant.

Every way I looked at it, the whole thing was entirely forbidden! Even to be seen with her would have compromised us both. Yet it was with her that I had had that blinding flash of love at first sight, that oceanic feeling I had reserved for God's appearance.

This experience of love at first sight is not entirely dissimilar to my big experience of years later, which we'll get to in due course. What love at first sight gives you, that merging with one person in an overflowing love and unity, my experience gave me later with the whole universe. Love at first sight gives a glimpse of that expansive blissful feeling, but two individuals are involved, and therefore two egos. Both you and that person continue to change. So it tends to fade with time and end with entanglement.

In my case, it left me more conflicted and confused than ever. I laugh now, but it only loaded more troubles onto my head. I longed for her to hold me in her arms and kiss me and fulfill my passionate fantasies. At the same time I wanted to be rid of her. But she persisted. The next time she came to the ballfield after school I made a point of leaving with the other boys so I wouldn't be trapped alone with her. But she came along with us. When she walked on one side of the road, I walked on the other. If she came to my side, I crossed over. I didn't want to talk with her. I didn't want to be near her. I especially didn't want to be *seen* near her.

One time she cornered me. She tried to talk to me, but I did not respond. I had this hearing problem. But mainly I was shy. The only thing I ever clearly heard her say was, "Are you not only deaf? Are you also dumb?! What's wrong with you?! Can't you even *speak* with a girl? Why won't you say even one word to me?" I did not answer. I did not know *what* to say to a girl!

Then she began to tease me.

I told my mother this girl was teasing me. To my dismay, Mother laughed. "I will talk with her," she said.

The next time I met this girl she taunted me all the more: "Hey, little boy, who tattle-tales to his mommy!"

I was so conflicted that I was afraid she might give up on me and stop coming entirely, but thankfully she didn't. I didn't know what I wanted. Once for two weeks I didn't see her and I felt horribly bereft.

The whole thing reached a head one day when we met on the edge of the village. We were standing there silent, awkward, not touching one another. To me it was enough just to be in her presence. Though at war within myself, it was still magic. She must have been giving all the signals and I must have been missing each and every one of them. I laugh now that I doubt I ever spoke a single full sentence to her.

We were about to part when she reached into her pocket and took out a small white handkerchief with handmade lace around the edges. She gave it to me. It seemed something of great emotion for her, giving me her hankie. I was so innocent in those years that I didn't know what to do with it. I held it awkwardly between two fingers, then I put it in my pocket and we just continued what we were doing, standing alone together, just looking at one another. Then we returned to the village, she to her place, me to mine.

Why had she given me that hankie? I hadn't a clue. Not a clue! Boys more clever than me knew about such things—that girls did this as a sign of their love, as I later came to know.

When I got home, that hankie was like a burning fire in my pocket. Where could I hide it? I had to do something with it. I was terrified my mother or father would find it and ask me where I got a girl's hankie. The first night I hid it balled up in my shirt. But we all slept in one room and it was bound to be discovered, the thought of which terrified me. I hardly slept that night.

In the morning, I went to the temple where I used to challenge God to appear. Everybody thought I was going to give a prayer. I went to the very room where I went daily for my saintly duty, the very place I hoped to encounter God, and I stuffed that girl's hankie in a corner, in a crack up by the roof. It was my hidden, forbidden secret, whose meaning was beyond my capacity of understanding, but whose import I knew to be tremendous.

Until then I had seen a hankie only in the hands of my mother. She used to take her coins and small rupee notes and she kept them tied in her hankie, which she then tucked into a fold of her clothing close to her bosom. When she went to market, she would produce it like magic from her intimate apparel to pay the vegetable dealer and when she bought rice. Sometimes she would buy me a sweet. She would take out some coins or a one- or two-rupee note, then tie the hankie again and tuck it back into the mysterious motherly folds of her clothing.

So for me the hankie was related to money—and nothing else.

I thought, "Why has this girl given me her hankie? Is it because she thinks I belong to rich parents? Could it be she wants me to return it with some money?

This made me further lose interest in her.

In the end, some short time later, when I saw her kissing some other boy, you know what I felt? Glad to be rid of her! Good riddance!

CHAPTER 6

WRESTLING FOR SURVIVAL

Getting rid of this girl, getting her out of my mind, didn't mean that I had overcome the sexual urge, or that I became a goody-goody. It is rather that I began to enjoy myself on my own, as boys of that age will, if you get my meaning. Perhaps you can imagine the war going on inside me.

My solution was to channel my physical energy and sexual urges into wrestling. Wrestling sort of saved me. While hockey and other group sports left me at a disadvantage because of my hearing, you don't need hearing to wrestle, just physical strength and a keen intelligence.

Our coach at school was strict. He worked us hard. Even when it was burning hot, he wouldn't let us drink water during training. He wanted to toughen us like leather. After practice I would go home and fall into bed. My mother would have to wake me for my evening meal. I devoted every available waking hour to building up my body. It is in my nature that no matter what I do, I do it all the way.

At this time the famous wrestler, who also became a Bollywood movie star, Dara Singh, became my hero. He was a monster and I wanted to be just like him. I became fascinated by his physique and everything about him. I thought about him day and night—while wrestling, while at school, while other kids would have been thinking of girls. I was grooming myself to be the next Dara Singh, the great Bollywood hero!

Looking back now, I am astounded by the firm determination, the focus with which I trained my body. My muscles became like iron. My mind was quick. I knew all the moves. I could get out of any hold and pin my opponent down with brute strength and cunning.

Every year just after the monsoon ended we had a village fair, during which there were wrestling matches. It happened in a muddy field and people would gather, local people, women and men, the men to watch and wrestle and the women to watch and clap. Everywhere were little knots of children. People came just to enjoy themselves. For a few years running I became famous in this tiny world of these village fairs. Sometimes they would pit two people against me. A crowd would gather to see the deaf kid with a body like Dara Singh's win over all opponents. Though I didn't actually win every match, that was my reputation, and it was great fun.

One day a group of two or three older boys from my village convinced me to go with them to what they said was going to be a fair in a small town not far away. They must have been in their early twenties and I was all of sixteen. It turned out not to be the usual fair such as was common in those days, with families, games, rides and all. What they brought me to turned out to be a professional wrestling match.

The wrestling happened in a big field. Two or three fights would be going on at any one time, each surrounded by a knot of a hundred jeering men, most of whom were drunk. It had the atmosphere of a cockfight. They were there to see people smash and be smashed and to gamble on the outcome.

These guys who brought me arranged for me to wrestle with a guy who was some five or six inches taller than me. Since I was such a big hit in my home village, and used to fight two people at once, at first I was flattered they thought he was a good match. But then I looked more closely at him and he was much older than me. He looked tough and hard and mean. I was a new boy, a rookie. Never gone much out of my village. I asked the guys who had brought me there to find me someone my own age, someone matching me. He was a full-grown man, huge and hulking. How could I ever wrestle with him?

But they knew him. "He's a friend," they told me. "He's our man. He will not harm you. Don't be afraid—just go and wrestle him. You'll do just fine."

I had no reason to disbelieve them. They were good people, these guys from my village. Since they had brought me there to wrestle, which was an honor for a kid like me, to go with these big boys to this real match, it showed they had confidence I could do it. So how could I now refuse?

What I didn't know, and was too naive to guess, was that they may have had hidden motives. I knew that the winner of the match didn't get a ribbon, but got to pass the hat. If it's a good match, it can be quite lucrative. But how was I to know that they might have made a deal with this gorilla to share the money he got by beating me, that they could then abandon me in that town and all go out drinking on the proceeds of my defeat?

Since I had no reason to doubt or refuse them, I began to wrestle. But I realized almost immediately that I'd been told some lie, and that I would not only be defeated: this colossus might even do me serious harm. So I began to make it look as if I was wrestling, but really I was just attempting to save my skin. To come into his grip—to fall into his clutches—would have been the end. He would make a mess of me—maybe even kill me! So I danced around him pretending to wrestle, just to show the people, just to save face. I played the clown, taunting this monster—but from a safe distance. Some minutes passed.

At no time was he bothered by my antics, my strategy for surviving this ordeal. He knew all he had to do was wait for me to tire myself out. Then he could come in for the kill. Wrestling, while it is a contest of muscle, is even more a contest of minds. That is why the weaker man can sometimes win, by pure cunning. But now I knew I was doomed. It was like a chess game whose outcome was already clear. As the superior player, he clearly understood this from the beginning. He was like a cat playing with a mouse, a cobra waiting for his moment to strike. I realized the longer this thing continued, the more tired I would be, and the worse I would get pummeled in the end.

The moment I realized this, I got a crazy notion. It was impromptu on my part, entirely unpremeditated, even unconscious: it welled up from some unknown source, but I sort of attacked him. I took hold of his wrist and pulled his arm with a short, firm tug. Normally this should have riled the beast into a frenzy of revenge, but what actually happened shocked me.

He made some awkward attempt to come after me, then he simply stopped. He just stood still. I started dancing around him, trying to stay out of his reach, but he just stood there, looking at his arm, which was dangling by his side as if dead.

"My shoulder is loosened," he said. "Look at it! It's not moving. It has come out. I can't move my arm."

I neither believed nor disbelieved him. It could be a trick. There was a referee, who managed the wrestling matches to ensure the fight was clean and to make sure no one got killed. He thought maybe this guy had simply gotten tired of fighting me. A tall man can easily get tired. So he came to my opponent. "Come on," he prodded. "Only a few minutes more. Then I'll stop the match and declare you winner."

"I am not lying," he said. "Look at it! My shoulder has loosened. It's dislocated. I cannot move my arm."

The crowd, drunken with liquor—drunk with the anticipation of my bloody pummeling—was jeering him now, thinking he was making some excuse not to play, or perhaps trying to lure me close enough so he could pounce. Finally, when he swore on the name of God that he couldn't move his arm, people finally understood that something had really happened.

The moment I realized that he truly was unable to wrestle me more and that I had won, I started dancing around him, taunting him with confidence, knowing he couldn't come after me.

I was declared the winner, and went around to collect the money, as was the custom in those days. The crowd was ecstatic at this David and Goliath win. They were throwing money at me— one- and two-rupee notes—congratulating me and patting me on the back. That day I went home with quite a tidy sum.

CHAPTER 7

AN ENGINEERING ADMISSION

When I had finished class twelve, it was time for me to gain admission to college. So my father took me and two of my classmates to Amritsar. We were friends from the village, each apprehensive of leaving for the big city, so we thought we'd go together, gain admission together, and attend the same classes.

You can imagine Amritsar in the eyes of three kids from a tiny rural village: huge, swirling, crowded, and chaotic. As chance had it, both of my friends were also called Vikram. Since all people of the Sikh religion have the surname Singh, there were two Vikram Singhs in one rickshaw and the third Vikram Singh and my father in another.

We were headed to a college that catered to village boys such as ourselves, which would offer us easy admission. All that we boys could possibly aspire to, for the smartest and best students amongst us, was a Bachelor of Science, a BSc. And those at the top of the class could perhaps hope to become a secondary school science teacher in some village or other. No one could even dream of anything higher. Most would go back to their farms and work the land. We were yet to wear proper pants. We still wore pajamas and kurtas. Maybe we had chappals, but we also still ran around barefoot.

So we were on our way, the three Vikram Singhs along with my father, riding in two rickshaws through the mad confusion of streets in the big city when out of the crowd came a familiar face, calling out my father's name. It was a former schoolteacher of mine. What he was doing in that huge city I do not know. And how it happened that in all that confusion he saw us still to this day seems a miracle.

We stopped and he asked my father what we were doing in Amritsar and where we were going. When my father told him he was bringing us three boys to gain admission to college and mentioned which college we were headed to, the schoolteacher objected vehemently. He knew what kind of student I was. Back in 8th standard, which was considered an important year because of certain tests you have to take, he offered tuition to us kids at night, in various subjects.

Sometimes I would challenge him. He would be writing a question on the board for us students to solve, and I would take pleasure in solving the problem and calling out the answer before he was even finished writing. Sometimes he'd get angry, but not really. If my friends laughed at me he would reprimand them. "Don't laugh," he would tell them. "None of you have his capabilities." So he knew my potential.

That is why he objected when my father mentioned what college we were headed to. "That's OK for these other two," he told my father. They had also been his students. "But for this one," and he pointed at me, "it isn't."

He said I should go to this other college, which we all knew of but could never dream of attending, a college at an entirely higher level. Not everybody could gain admission there, only brilliant students of rich families. My father objected, but when my schoolteacher said he knew people at this other college and that he would come along to help, my father could not refuse. So we changed course and went first to this other college to see about my admission.

How different the course of my life would have been had we not chanced into this schoolteacher in the mad confusion of streets that day in Amritsar!

When we got to the college the admissions officer asked me what degree I was interested in pursuing. I was still thinking like a peasant boy. I said "Bachelor of Science, BSc, Part I." This was the first step to that coveted job as a high school science teacher. My former teacher intervened.

"No!" he said. "You should take up engineering."

I mumbled something about how I didn't want that, how I wanted to become a high school teacher and not aim so high above my humble station as to even think of becoming an engineer.

We didn't have money. Nobody in our situation would even have in their minds to get into engineering. We thought to get into engineering people had to be very intelligent. They had to have had fancy tutors. They were city people. They belonged to rich families. Nobody from a village could even dream of doing an engineering degree. And besides, these elite colleges would never give admission to a village boy like me, still moving in pajamas and kurtas, and not yet started wearing pants.

When I put in my papers, there was a board of selectors sitting there, four professors, all men, dressed in suits, asking me questions, but of course I couldn't hear them. One of them looked at me and started laughing. He said, "He's wearing pajamas and chappals, how can we admit him to engineering college? He has no manners whatsoever."

I understood what he was saying from his gestures; I heard it, sort of. I'm quite good at lipreading and putting it together with body language to understand what people are saying. I was quite bold and resolute. I do not know where it came from. "Maybe you have failed to notice," I said, "but these pajamas are not fixed to my legs. They are not stuck to my bones like flesh. I don't see what this has to do with granting me admission!"

This time they all laughed at the audacity of my outburst. It must have impressed them. They proceeded to the interview.

Damned obvious though it was that I was hard of hearing, they found it amusing to fling questions at me and see me unable to answer, as if I was just too dumb.

I flashed back in anger, "It is painfully obvious to any intelligent being that if I cannot *hear* your questions, I cannot *answer* them. Either you ask your questions in writing or we can just stop this ridiculous interview." I said something to that effect. My tone was more like "Go to hell!"

The confidence of my delivery surprised even me. It must have impressed them. They began handing me questions in writing, most of which I could answer with ease. At the end of the process they offered me a seat.

But there was one last hurdle to my being admitted: the physical examination. I was afraid the medical officer would come to know that I was hard of hearing and reject me. It was enough that I wore pajamas and was obviously such a crude-mannered, rough-hewn country boy. Used to admitting the sons of big land-holders, doctors, lawyers, and politicians, that already would have been enough for this polished institution to reject me. I was deathly afraid that his coming to know of my hearing would prove my undoing.

The medical officer sat behind his big wooden desk. His two assistants in white smocks stood beside him with clipboards and pens and forms on the ready. He had me stand bare-chested before him. This was at the height of my wrestling career. My body was muscular and hard as nails. He began the examination by asking me if I was from Amritsar District. When I said yes, he joked with his assistants, "Only Amritsar District people are capable of such a body."

The doctor stood and approached me for the medical exam. He tried to pinch my stomach and my arm.

"You can't even pinch it!" he exclaimed.

And with that the exam was over. Before him stood an obviously healthy specimen. He never noticed anything about my hearing.

And so it was that I got into engineering college.

The other two Vikram Singhs gained admission to the college we were originally headed to. After college, one of them went back to farming. The other—and it is rather surreal: not only did he share my name, Vikram Singh, but he *became* what I was supposed to be. While I have fought most of my life to shake off the baba label, he went out of his way to take it on. It is his profession! It is what he does. It is his role in the world. He is known as Baba Vikram Singh.

Yes, in India being a baba is a proper profession. He is now quite famous in surrounding villages and people come to him. It is even reported that he gives boons, just like a baba is supposed to! If you want, I can show you his photo one day.

He's the *real* thing—not like me. To be a baba is to be a prisoner. Twenty-four seven. People have so many expectations about how babas are supposed to behave; it is worse than being a politician. People half expect their politicians to be crooked, to say one thing and do another. They expect them to be drunkards and do dirty deals. Not so for babas. They are supposed to be blemishless.

Every move you make is scrutinized. You are always safeguarding your reputation, and without your reputation you are nothing. By forcing the baba to act in a certain way, disciples rob the baba of his spontaneity. And what is a sage if he is not spontaneous? A baba cannot afford to be spontaneous, to be himself. He is too busy fulfilling a role, conforming to expectations. People expect so many things from those they look up to, like their saints, or even their artists. They demand that they conform.

Sartre refused to take his Nobel Prize because as the winner of such a prestigious award people would expect some particular way of life from him. He wanted to be free, and not have that load put upon him. I also want to be free, spontaneous. Babas are not allowed to have a drink. You see, I would not like to be the kind of baba who would drink stealthily. If I drink, I will do so openly.

CHAPTER 8

AN ENGINEER'S TRAINING

Within a few months I joined engineering college. Because of my hearing it would have been useless for me to attend lectures. So whatever I learned I got from books. And I never bought a book. I'd get hold of one from a friend a few days before the exam. "Just give me the book for a night," I'd say. I would take the book and sort of devour it. I had the ability to pick out the important ideas and facts and equations. If some line attracted my attention, or some chapter title, I would start reading from there. In two, three, or four days I would be prepared for the exam—and I always passed. Never did I bother standing first in my class. I aimed for a 60 or a 70, right in the middle—neither failing nor coming first. Just enough so my father wouldn't scold me. I did not want more than that.

I was living in a hostel with other boys from the engineering college. While they spent their days in class and at the library, I spent most of my time in the gym. And even when I was in my room, I was always doing sit-ups and pushups.

The other boys in the hostel, mostly from quite fine backgrounds, laughed at me: "He's an engineering student and we never see him read a book! He's always doing sit-ups!" Everything about me must have seemed coarse to them.

One of these boys—he lived directly across the hall—became my closest friend and was to have a profound impact upon my life. He was a few years elder to me.

He was everything I was not. He was a thin man. I was a strong man. He was sophisticated, lean, and intellectual. He wore spectacles and would never speak loudly. To him I must have appeared like an uncut crystal, a village boy, rough around the edges, a wrestler. His passion was ideas; mine was building body mass. He looked literary and fine.

Somehow, we struck up a friendship. I was impressed by him. He came from a famous Punjabi literary background. His father was closely associated with renowned Punjabi writer and thinker, Gurbaksh Singh Preetlari; they were like a single family. Our friendship must have been the attraction of opposites.

One day we were sitting in his room and he was telling me about all the modern thinkers who don't believe in God. "Many great men do not believe in God," he told me. "Even Prime Minister Nehru doesn't. And he is not alone, many of the great thinkers of all times have been atheists."

I must have known that it was possible not to believe in God, but back in the village in those days *everybody* believed in God. I knew that Christians had their god. Muslims believed in some other god; Hindus believed in any number—but I'd never thought I'd actually meet someone who didn't believe in *any* god.

He was speaking so freely and convincingly of those who believed in no god that I had to ask him, "Well, do you believe in God?"

He laughed and said, "No way! Of course not."

My face must have grown pale. Things began to spin. I was shaken to the core. I was so impressed by my friend, I so looked up to him, and he said he didn't believe in God!

It felt as if someone had thrown me into the sky. I lost myself entirely. And when I landed back on the ground, he was all in all for me, like a guru, my guide. From the surface, and maybe for him, we were friends. But from the inside I knew I was not his friend, but more like his disciple. He was everything I was not, and I admired him for it. You could say before this I was looking for some absolute in God. Now I found it in my friend.

And so it was, after all I'd been through—the whole saint thing, the searching, my challenging God to appear—that I became an atheist. There couldn't be a god because I tried so hard and nobody came. So I thought, "Fuck all that restraint, entangled by my mother and sisters and everyone who thought I was a baba. Who needs it?"

I went to the other extreme. It has always been my nature to go to the other extreme, no matter what the situation. So I started abusing everything religious. Whenever I'd meet someone who still had God, or the gods, on his or her mind, no matter what their belief, I'd call them damn fools, knowing full well that none of them had ever had any evidence for their faith. None had experience of their god. They were like a herd of cows. When people would come around collecting money for the anniversary of this or that saint, I'd say, "Get away from me! I don't believe in your bloody saint, I'm not interested. Leave me!"

I began to read about communism, all those who were against God, those who didn't believe in God. Rationalist philosophers like J. Paul Sartre, like Camus. Like Che Guevara.

We Sikh men don't cut our hair; we wear it piled on our heads, covered by a turban. For fear of my father's wrath, I did not yet dare cut my hair or free my head of the turban. But I wore my beard like Lenin's.

And so it was that I became a communist, a leftist—whatever you want to call it. I moved in leftist circles. I looked like one and I dressed like one too. I moved amongst them, read their books, and thought like one. In other words, as I see it now, I took on the *persona* of a communist—whatever that meant amongst the young men of the Punjab at that time. Looking back, I now see that I had worn out my saintly persona only to take on the next. In other words, I took on the adjective *communist* and began with all sincerity to play the role of the goody-goody communist in my dress, my speech, and in the way I acted. You could say it was a fashion.

I don't think this brought me any closer to myself. No matter what the adjective, the role, the ideology, no matter how you present yourself to the world: if it fits an image or a label in the minds of others it starts a feedback loop. The others will inevitably start to subtly yet steadily coerce you into acting in such a way as to fit that label. They will expect you to conform to *their* image, *their* idea, *their* expectations for the adjective they place upon you. This will naturally and perhaps unconsciously make you feel obliged to take on this adjective, this expectation from society, and fulfill it. And as soon as you do this—or to the extent you do this—you are not free. When you find yourself reflecting such an image back to the world, you will have become just what they thought you should be, conforming to that label they put on you. When this happens, you have already lost your way on your path to yourself, which it is your duty to pursue, no matter what the obstacles.

I used to go to my friend's family's house. They lived in the village that was created by the great writer Gurbaksh Singh Preetlari. It was called Preet Nagar, the City of Love. He created a whole village based on his ideas and he invited famous actors, writers, thinkers, and artists to come and live there. It was a great experiment. They all lived there together. Even Nehru came there to pay homage.

I spent most of the breaks and holidays during my college years at my friend's house in this village. In the evenings I'd eat with the family in the kitchen. They were very open people. Some kind of different people. They had a different way of living. I would go there and I would be sitting in their kitchen, with my friend's mother or his sisters, or sometimes somebody else—we'd be sitting and eating, sitting right on the floor, and sometimes he would come in, Gurbaksh Singh would walk into the kitchen and he'd be standing there.

It was as if your British poet Wordsworth, or Walt Whitman, was standing there live as day. It was like meeting Emerson. And he was nothing less. He was no less than the great Bengali poet Rabindranath Tagore. Tagore got the Nobel Prize because he translated his *Gitanjali* into English. Gurbaksh Singh never did. He didn't care about English. He said one must live and work and die in one's mother tongue. Still, he was famous all over India.

Sometimes my friend would say, "Let's go see the great writer," and we would go to him. Because my friend's family was like second to his own, he would see us. He was usually in his study. Gurbaksh Singh first introduced me to Whitman's *Leaves of Grass*. He wrote about Goethe. He wrote about many French and German and English writers as well. I got my first initiation into the Western thinkers through him, and through his works.

And so it was that for the four years of college I lived under the influence and in the company of my friend. Under his tutelage I became an atheist and refused God to my heart's content.

We finished engineering college at the same time. I put in an extra push at the end and came in near the top of my class. All the top students of my class, myself included, got temporary jobs as assistants in a place where a dam was being built. But I only stayed there for twenty-five days, until I got a telegram from Chandigarh saying I had been selected to be an SDO, a Sub-Divisional Officer, an unusually high position for someone just out of engineering college, especially for a deaf student! The others all remained there as I took on my new position. With time, my friend got posted to some other place.

CHAPTER 9

A MARRIAGEABLE AGE

It was while at my first posting that the time came for me to marry. I was going to my home village whenever I could get away, and it was there one day that I ran into that girl with the hankie, the one with whom I'd experienced that love at first sight. Only this time I wasn't a shy young boy. Now I was a young man with a very bright future, an important man, an Officer of the Punjab Public Works Department.

I got it into my mind that I wanted to marry her. Since I was now a communist, I didn't believe in the usual rituals and all the other societal conventions. I didn't care about our difference in caste. So I had my sisters go on my behalf and ask for her hand. This was highly unusual. Normally, one would go to the *parents* of the girl and not the girl herself. Also, it would be the boy's father or some respected intermediary who would go—definitely not the boy's sisters. But that is what I did. I had my sisters go to the girl to ask for her hand.

The girl, obviously more conventional than I, said, "Don't ask me! Go ask my parents."

When my sisters reported this back to me, I was greatly encouraged. At least she hadn't outright refused me; she must have still liked me too.

So I sent my sisters to the mother.

The mother said if the father said it was OK it would be OK.

So I sent my sisters to him, but he grew furious.

He said, "The boy is hard of hearing. He can't hear! No family of his own caste wants to give them a daughter and now they want mine?!"

This was a great blow to my ego. A girl's family refusing *me*, an engineer and Officer with the PWD?

Both humiliated and determined, I decided then and there that I would give myself one week to find another wife and to finalize it. My goal was to be engaged within one week!

So I put the word out, and my friends were all suggesting that I marry this girl or that. Some big people tried to act as go-between. I told everyone if you know a girl, show her to me. Somebody showed me this girl. Someone else, that girl. They were pressing me. Then a friend told me of a girl from a big landholding family. I said, OK, show me that girl. So I went there. It was a good solid farming family. I liked that girl. I just liked her, so I thought it would be OK to marry her.

While I was looking for a wife, I was also going to my friend's village. My friend's sister was also of my age, perhaps two or three years younger. I found out later that she was in love with me and was interested in marrying. The whole family had spoken of it. But because she was my friend's sister, and because I had spent so much time in their house living like a member of the family, she was practically like my own sister. It never crossed my mind to think of her in any other way. We ate together, we walked together, we practically lived together—like brother and sister. My friend was like my guru. How could I have thought of his sister in that way?

One day it all became obvious. It was just when I had selected this other girl and before I had finalized it. I found out later the whole family was hoping I would marry my friend's sister and be one of them. After some time it became clear. Her mother told me something. Another common friend suggested we should marry, all very indirectly. Even the Great Writer himself was in on it. I tried to entertain the possibility, flattered that such an illustrious family would have me as one of their own. But I just couldn't imagine it with my friend's sister.

It just so happened that I was in their village on a short leave from my job. My position included a car, which was rare in those days when only VIPs had cars. So I was in their village with my car, and my friend had to go back to his place of posting. I offered to drive him there. His sister asked if she could come along, and I was somehow thick enough that I didn't think much of it. I offered to drive her back home after we dropped her brother off.

We dropped my friend off and were for the first time alone in the car. It was unusual back then, especially in rural India, for a young boy and a young girl to be alone together. She didn't talk much, but she must have been hinting. But I still couldn't see her as anything other than a sister. I was blithely speaking of what was obviously on my mind, my plans to marry, how after I dropped her off I would go finalize my engagement to this other girl. We were forty-five minutes from her village, and she must have been thinking that this was our last chance. It must have been excruciating for her.

As we neared her village, she became silent. I turned, and tears were rolling down her cheeks. For the first time I could feel just how in love she was, and what a tragedy this was for her. She started crying. I felt sad for her, but there was nothing I could do. Because of my hearing and because I was driving, we couldn't even talk. She produced a pen and paper from somewhere. She wrote something and handed it over to me. "It is OK," she wrote. "I will get over it. This, too, shall pass. Don't worry. I was in love with you, but it cannot be." Something like that.

It did something to my relationship with my friend as well. He told me later that he had long thought his sister and I would make a good match. He had even tried to bring us together in his own subtle way, but in my own cocoon of self, my deafness like bales of cotton, I had missed every clue. And remember, at the time he was like a teacher to me, a guru, he knew me better than I knew myself. At least that's how I saw it.

From the moment I became an atheist under his tutelage I believed in his superior wisdom. He must have known on what a pedestal I put him. Maybe he found it amusing. He was wise enough to know that if he told me that his sister and I would make a good pair I would be unduly influenced. If his sister and I were to be united, it would have to happen on its own. It didn't happen, and I married that other girl.

CHAPTER 10

MARRIED LIFE

After a short engagement, my wife and I were married. Since I was then a communist and an atheist, I did not believe in all the religious rituals and conventions surrounding marriage. So we kept it to a minimum, just enough to keep our families off our backs. That said, the marriage did what it was supposed to. From the day of our marriage we were joined on the deepest level. Two lives were joined into one. And they remained so until about two years ago, when my wife died. But even though our lives were so deeply entwined, we never really felt comfortable with each other.

Like many Indian couples, when we married we hardly knew each other, and from the first we were a bad fit. When I felt hot, she was cold. When I wanted tea, she didn't. If I wanted the fan on, she wanted it off. This is not to say we didn't love each other. We not only loved each other. We loved each other and we hated each other—both with a passion.

My wife's father was a very rational person, and he passed this on to his daughter. It helps explain why she was so willing to marry an avowed and outspoken atheist. When we married, I was in active revolt against everything that the birthmark on my arm had brought me. But one's earliest imprint is still the hardest to wash out. Even during my most fervent communist period, when I would lash out at anything with even a whiff of religion, I still had this baba thing in me like a nest of fleas, which flared up from time to time. Acting like a baba, talking like a baba, even believing myself to be a baba has, as the Christians would say, been my cross to bear. It persisted even when I was an avowed and vocal atheist and had become a communist! What a tangle of contradictions we are.

My wife and I used to joke that I was somewhat schizophrenic and that she was completely hysterical. Was I literally schizophrenic? Probably not. The psychologist R. D. Laing said mystics and schizophrenics find themselves deep in the same ocean. The difference is that the mystics learn to swim while the schizophrenics drown. All mystics are probably somewhat schizophrenic. Just as all schizophrenics are somewhat mystics—at least in seed form, in their potential.

Anyway, that's to get ahead of ourselves. The point here is that it was psychologically impossible for my wife and I to fit well together. I was already lost into my own self, and she was already hysterical, which went back to her life before we were married.

India gained independence from the British in 1947, two years before I took birth. It also brought partition, the splitting of British India into two countries, India and Pakistan. Nowhere was the exodus of Hindus to India and Muslims to Pakistan worse than in our Punjab, which was split right down the middle. Over a million people died in the exodus.

When my wife's parents fled Pakistan, they lost everything. They came with the rags on their backs to a place they didn't know and bought sandy land for cheap. Her father, who prior to Partition had been the son of a prosperous merchant and was set to follow in his father's footsteps, started farming in order to feed the family. The land was hard and unforgiving, and her father became much the same. He put his kids to work and almost killed them with heavy labor. My wife had to go from before dawn to well into the night. Apart from the hard work in the fields, she also had to prepare food for everyone in the family as well as for the hired hands, when they had them, and for guests. She never had a moment to herself and could never do what she wanted, not for five minutes together in the day. Even though they turned that sandy soil into a prosperous farm by the time we were married, it left its effect upon the psychology of the children, including my wife. She was a rebel. She both loved her father and hated him— at the same time. When we married, all this got transferred from her father onto me.

It was hard for me to understand at first where all this was coming from. Remember, we hardly knew each other when we married. Naturally it upset me, and though it took me some time, I got to the root of the problem—it was actually painfully obvious—that it was all about her father. Imagine your new wife coming to you and doing nothing but cursing and crying and ranting against her father, and then turning it on you! Because the rants directed against me were really aimed at her father, there was a hopelessness to her struggle.

I tried to be kind, but it wasn't easy since I was now the target of her anger. From my side, it wasn't so much love at first sight as it was *sympathy* at first sight. In retrospect I could have done more to comfort her and calm her nervous tensions.

Part of the problem with our marriage, especially at the beginning, was that I told my wife everything, whatever was on my mind. So I told her all about the girl I had wanted to marry from my village, the one with whom I'd felt that love at first sight, the one whose father had rejected me for being deaf. After telling her all about it and what I'd felt for that girl, my wife would grow wildly jealous whenever I went to my village—even if she came with me! It did not help that ever since I had become an atheist I used to enjoy looking at other girls—just to be carefree, to enjoy, to make a split with my goody-goody past. Sometimes I did things just to stick it to the saint, to prove I was now on the other side. I didn't see why being married should make me stop looking at other girls.

Hysterical people have the ability to concentrate an enormous amount of energy on the smallest point of detail. They tend to obsess. Schizophrenic people are always discovering connections between things: they see what is happening in general. She never missed when I was looking at some other girl, and she always grew furious.

At the time of our marriage I was posted as the Sub-Divisional Officer in a town right on the Pakistani border. It was a good position. It came with a car and a driver, a bungalow to live in, servants, and all the perks of being an Officer. My new wife came to live with me there. We stayed there for five or six years.

One of my first jobs was to coordinate with the Pakistani side in the construction of huge concrete pillars along the mutually

agreed upon border between our two countries so they could never be disputed. Every day I would go with my sub engineers, my
junior engineers, my road inspectors, earth movers, cement mix-
ers, trucks full of reinforcing rods, and a few flatbed trucks of
migrant workers to do the work, and we would go to the border
along with senior military brass with their maps and transits.
With an armed military escort we would meet our Pakistani
counterparts at the border. After a section of border was mapped
out to our mutual agreement, we'd plot the exact placement of
these huge and unmovable pillars. Each side built every other
pillar. They are there to this day.

You'd never guess it now with the tension between our two
countries, but the armies of both sides would sometimes plan a
party together at the border. The Officers in both military and
civil service were allowed to bring their wives. My wife used to
love mixing with the wives of the military commanders and those
of my higher ups, from whom she sometimes gleaned useful gos-
sip. It made her feel somehow special and offered a short respite
from her troubled existence.

CHAPTER 11

BECOMING ANCHORLESS

Shortly after our marriage, I took my wife to where my friend was posted so they could get to know one another. Usually my friend and I would give each other our undivided attention. Now I had to tend to and care for my wife. Wives don't usually want their husband subordinate to anyone, nor to divide them with someone else. We were new together and she was insecure, transferring both her love and hate for her father upon me. She demanded the whole of my attention and would become quarrelsome if she didn't get it.

My friend and I were used to sleeping in beds in the same room and talking deep into the night. He was like a guru to me, and I used to practically serve him. Now I slept with my wife in a separate room. In the morning, when we came out from our room my friend was upset and didn't hide it. He clearly had been brewing on something all night. There must have been something in my behavior. I had never seen him like that. My wife and I left well before noon.

Later, my friend wrote me a letter. In it he said how he'd never thought to see me acting like this, like such a non-person. He told me I had thrown my life away.

At the time, I hadn't a clue why he was condemning me so. It must have been because of his sister. My wife and I were so mismatched that we quarreled constantly. He must have been upset at the chance I'd squandered to marry his sister—and to be his brother-in-law.

At the end of the letter he wrote, "Let us not meet again—at least not for some time." He also wrote, "I never thought you were such a dunce."

He closed the chapter for me.

There was no question of my going there again.

My friend had been my anchor all those years, the one I could turn to, and when I got married I lost that anchor. I could no longer go to him to discuss the course of my life and what I should do. It would have been natural for married life to become the next anchor. But my wife and I didn't match. What happened was this: my soul went in search of my next anchor and couldn't find it.

For many, work becomes the anchor. It defines one's place in society and comes with a readymade answer for why you have come to this earth. If I am a shoemaker, I am here to make shoes and with the money I earn feed my family. If I'm a district engineer, I'm here to oversee the building of large public works. One's work generally determines one's place in society, which is different for a shoemaker and a senior district engineer. It determines how many people call you "Sir." Each profession comes with a ready-made set of goals based on one's station in life. It gives many the reason for why they came to this earth. And since it is given, ready-made, most don't question it. They glide into their role, their place on the stage, and it fits them like a foot gliding into a boot—or, in my case, like a bird getting locked into a cage.

The problem was that not only did my marriage offer me no safe harbor, but my work put me into conflict, at first with myself and then with my bosses at Headquarters. I was overseeing large projects, like roads, bridges, and dams. I would put out for bids from construction companies and was expected to take bribes and work them up the line to my superiors. Those looking for favors gave gifts. It was part of the culture. There was booze and there were women and all manner of temptation—all of which I was expected to partake in. Lots of dirty dealing. In the position I occupied, one is tied into a web of corruption into which one is continually sandwiched between one's superiors and one's subordinates, with each depending on the other to keep the rupees moving up the line. Everybody is enmeshed. It was telling lies day and night, doing this, that—everything. Perhaps you can imagine. There were some low actions. People supplying girls to their senior officers.

Was I tempted by the perks my position offered me? You bet! But I was also innocent—not *that* innocent—but innocent all the same. I could neither get rid of that saint sitting in my head nor get into the job. I wanted to quit, but how could I? No one from my village had ever reached so high a position. I saw no solution. Things were moving me to a point of despair. I would have loved to talk with my friend. Why did my friend treat me like that? Why did he say, Let us not meet?

And so it was, in my anchorless state, that a darkness began to stir. I became a misfit on the job. I began quarreling with my seniors. Whatever they instructed me to do, they were always expecting this and that thing in return. They were nasty and selfish people. What I really wanted was to tell them all to go to hell!

All of this led me to a crisis, an inevitable and even necessary crisis. I knew I was a mess, that I knew nothing about who I was. And not knowing who I was, how could I know what I was supposed to do, how to conduct my life? I began to think deeply about this life and what it is all about. With the help of my friend, I had gotten rid of God. With God, there would have been some universal standard by which one could judge one's actions, especially in answering the question of what was good and what was bad. But if there was no God, no divine rules, no tablet with the commandments chiseled in stone, if there was no universal standard, then how could one really know what was good and what was bad? If good and bad were relative, subject to society's shifting standards, differing from country to country, religion to religion, and changing through historical time, then why shouldn't I enjoy like my colleagues were enjoying—gaining money, drinking, having fun, women, all? Nothing held them back. What the hell! Why shouldn't I also enjoy life to the hilt?

Was this life just like a balloon, like a bubble, that one day would pop, leaving nothing in its place? Was there nothing that persisted? Was there really no larger meaning in life? This life is short—I had come twenty-something years before, and in forty I would go. And once I was dead, what would happen to that voice inside my head telling me to do this and not to do that? Wouldn't it pop with the balloon? Why not give in to temptation? What *is* this sense of good and bad? So what, in this short span of life, this bubble on a stream, which one day will vanish like a forgotten dream!? Why not try to squeeze all the enjoyment out of this bubble of existence before it pops?

Nothing was stopping me from enjoying like the others. In fact, I was being forced into it from all sides and if anything getting into trouble for resisting. If I only let myself, I could have it all—money, drink, women...

I asked myself how best to live this short span of life, this blink of an eye. Some say there is a god. What is that god? Was he invented just to get people to behave themselves? What really is good and bad? Who am I? A mere balloon? Some day I will explode into the space of nothingness, or whatever it is into which we dissolve when we die. And what is it into which we dissolve? What is spacetime? Where does it end? And what lies beyond that?

If only I could penetrate this question, Who am I?—then, I thought, I would know how I was supposed to live my life.

Such a simple question: Who am I? Yet the answer to a question reflects the level at which the question is asked. On the surface I could have answered, I am Vikram. I was born in such-and-such a year at such-and-such a place. I am an engineer. I could produce a birth certificate and diplomas to prove it, and leave it at that.

But what if I took it on a deeper level, if I went beneath my given name and my role in the world—as a son, a father, an engineer, a husband, a good man or a bad? *Who* was asking the question? *I* was the one asking. But who was that I that was asking?

The answers to a single question can be many.

A boy asks his mother: "How did I come into this world?" If she is wise, she will answer according to his age and reflect his level of understanding. Her answer will be correct for the time at which it was asked.

When he is young, too young for school, and the boy asks his mother how did he come into this world, the mother might say, "A giant bird dropped you in the cabbage patch and I picked you up." This answer is bound to satisfy such a young boy.

He grows up a little more and becomes dissatisfied with the answer. Again, he asks the same question. His mother says something else.

A little later he asks the question again. His mother, now a bit embarrassed, says, "Go play outside and look at nature; look at the plants and the animals." She tries to make him understand. He goes and looks at a bird catching a fly on the wing. He sees a bee on a flower. He sees the cow munching grass. What has all that has to do with him and how he came into the world?

Again, he grows up. He reaches puberty. It bothers him that he does not know from where he came, and again asks the same question. This time his father overhears.

"Go," his father says, laughing, "and find a wife. Then you will *automatically* know!"

Through experience there is nothing left to question, just like that young man who takes some girl into his bed. Then he will *know* how he came into this world. This also goes for spiritual things too. These are not ideas in which one must have faith. These are matters of experience. If your experience is authentic, you will be left with no questions. And if you have no questions, nothing will be left unanswered

But back then, I was full of questions that had no answers. I was adrift, having left that saint behind and having been left behind by my friend. I was married, but we did not get on. And now I was being tempted by the perks of my job.

Perhaps it was inevitable that my inside problems would manifest themselves on the outside. I was fighting with myself, but soon I was fighting with my superiors. When I wanted to, I could do the work of five Sub-Divisional Officers. When I was not in the mood, I would be quarreling with my superiors—especially when I knew they wanted money. How good they all looked from the outside, "public servants" doing their jobs, but how greedy they were for gain.

And so it was that things came to a head.

One day my senior was supposed to come to where I was posted to meet a high government official for some sort of inspection. It was about a bridge we were building. For some reason, at the last moment my superior couldn't make it. Perhaps he was sick, or his car broke down—I cannot now recall. But when that big government official came all the way from Pathankot and my superior wasn't there, it became clear that the purpose of their meeting was the passing of a goodly sum of dirty money. And they wanted me to step in and take my superior's place in the transaction.

Sometimes I can be quite bold. I have a power that seems to know no end. I got into an argument with this official, with the big man from Headquarters in Pathankot, and I ended up lecturing him on how to behave. It devolved into a shouting match. He told me to shut up. Then I told him to shut up. He must have been scared of me. I did not threaten him, but in the middle of it all he told his driver to ready his jeep and they sped away.

I was not this old man you see today. I had been a wrestler. I was twenty-seven and I think it safe to say I exuded a certain physical, almost menacing power. Like other Sikh men, I always had tucked into my belt the large knife we call *kirpan*; I also packed a revolver. It was something of a fashion in those days, amongst the young men of the Punjab.

I found out later he didn't go back to the city of Pathankot, where he was posted. Instead, he had his driver take him straight to Chandigarh, the capital, where the government Ministers and Secretaries were located. I know this because the next day a messenger came with an official letter from the Secretary in charge of the Public Works Department informing me that I had succeeded in getting myself suspended.

The first and immediate consequence of my suspension was that the bungalow where we had been living in all that style—the servants, the car and driver, everything, including my salary—was taken away. I had been the first and only boy from my village to become an engineer, let alone an Officer of the state government—and this despite my hearing problem and at such a young age! What a bright future stretched out before me! I was talked about. My whole village was proud of me. That was my successful engineer persona, and now I had thrown it all away. It must have looked as if I had gone off the rails. Nobody could understand. When people asked me what I would do now—and everybody was asking, pushing me—I had no answer.

Who could have possibly understood that within myself I was consumed with asking the fundamental questions pared down to the bone: Why did I come into this life? If the balloon will ultimately pop and this will all be gone, then how can it have meaning? Maybe I was driven forward by an intuition that there was something enduring, something behind all this coming and going, and I only had to crash through a barrier.

I told you my wife was a hysteric and I was something of a schizophrenic. Maybe it was because I couldn't hear that I have always tended to live in a sphere of my own. Maybe I always had more time than the common man to think without distractions.

After my suspension, my wife and son went first to my parents. Then they went to her parents. I was neither here nor there: sometimes, especially at the beginning, I would go to my parents', sometimes to hers. Later, there was an uncle in Chandigarh, and my sister's husband in another city. My brother was in Amritsar. I spent a few days here and a few days there.

When I got suspended, our first son was about a year old. We didn't know it yet—or at least I didn't—that my wife was pregnant again. Our second son was born at my in-law's house about six months into my suspension. But by then, her father couldn't stand the sight of me. I was no longer welcome. Exiled.

My father and father-in-law were equally tough on me, questioning what I was going to do with my life and how I would feed my children. We called my wife's father Hitler. My father we called the Police Inspector. Both were equally hard task-masters. I was labeled a rebel and a misfit. Even my mother, who never doubted that I was a saint, started calling me a misfit saint, convinced that I had gone bad. My father just called me a misfit.

I came to the point of despair. I was without my friend, my wife, my children. I was without God or Marx. I was for all intents and purposes no longer an engineer and certainly not a VIP with a bungalow, servants, a driver, and a car. I had no salary and no money. I was, and had, nothing. I was nowhere, floating, drifting with no safe harbor. My friend, he would always have advised me. But he was out of the picture. So I was left to myself. My questions were general, broad, and persistent: What to do with this life I was given? What was a goal worth striving for?

Yesterday, I came. Tomorrow, I will go. There are a few years in-between, a mere flash of light between two eternities of darkness. I was tempted by my job and the perks that it offered, but I was vexed by this voice perched inside my head telling me what I should and shouldn't do. "This is good," it whispers in one ear; "This is bad," it whispers in the other. Its business is to cleave the world in two as it discriminates between good and evil, good acts and bad. Everybody has a voice in their head, but it tells them different things. What is good to one might be evil to another. What happens to this voice inside my head when my ego—my me, my sense of I—one day pops? Will I then be nowhere? Could it be that all this could never have been? This whole life—could it be some kind of illusion? A sinking feeling would come over me. Is it possible, could it be, that all of this could never have been?

What is space? Where does it end? And what's beyond that? What is God, what people call God? What the hell is God? Who am I? Just like that balloon?

One of our Punjabi poets came close to expressing how I felt. He wrote, and I'll have to translate:

I am a zero,
Imprisoned in a cage, pacing.
Inside this emptiness
I am just going to and fro.

The poem went something like that. It expressed my position exactly. Someday my balloon will explode. I will die. Will that be the end? Will there be release when I die? My life had been stamped by that birthmark on my arm. I could no more take it off my arm than I could stop its influence. Even in my rebellion, in my repudiation of the whole damn thing, even when I became an atheist—it didn't matter. I was still under its influence. Forced, you could say, from behind, to ask those deeper questions about existence.

I kept returning to the idea that if there was no universal frame of reference, no absolute, then everything was just floating like a mirage, without foundation. And if nothing rests on solid ground why shouldn't I take advantage of my situation to enjoy like the others? Who's to say what is wrong and what is right? Where do these things come from, these values, if there is no permanency, if they are but a matter of consensus among transient beings on a planet revolving around some average-sized star in some random galaxy? And given that I don't know anything, what is the best way to live this short span of life?

A little over a year into my suspension I became ill. I was so far gone that I didn't noticed it myself. Someone told me I had turned yellow and must have jaundice. He told me people died from this, and I should get it checked by a doctor. But I refused. I was already dead, sort of. I didn't care. I had no regret. My attitude was, whatever will happen will happen.

I went to my brother's place in Amritsar. I had no place else to go. He was married, but his wife was in our village and he was living alone.

So I was living at my brother's place in Amritsar, and I had no money. He was feeding me. One day he gave me money to buy food, but instead I went out and bought some books on painting: *How to Draw*, something like that. I must have thought maybe I could become a painter. I didn't know what else to do. My brother was out working all day, and when he came home he quarreled with me. "You don't have any money," he screamed. "You are out of your job—maybe even out of your mind! You are eating from my hand, and spending money meant for food on books?"

How to explain that I was only trying to attach myself to something? My mind had lost the habit of attaching itself to anything. I was wondering what I was supposed to do. So I thought maybe I would paint.

A former classmate would sometimes come when I was staying at my brother's. He would stay a few days. Amritsar is a big city, surrounded by a ring road. I had so much energy, but it was not finding an outlet. He would take me out, just to dissipate my energy, as if I were a caged lion. We would walk the entire ring. We would circle Amritsar! Just so I could exhaust myself.

Somehow, the days were passing.

CHAPTER 12

AN AWAKENING

One day, something wonderful happened. My brother was away at work. It was midday. I took a chair and went out to the little balcony overlooking the street. When I sat down I was in a failed state, increasingly certain that I'd reached a dead end. I was in a surrendered position, you could say.

To truly describe what happened next is doomed to failure. Perhaps you could say that it was like that love at first sight. But while the experience of love at first sight is a certain merging with one other human being in love, this time it was with the entire universe. If God is love, as the mystics sometimes say, I was merging with that. But I'd rather not put a label on it.

It is rather like what Saint Augustine said about time. When someone asked him what time is, he said, "What then is time? If no one asks me, I know what it is. If I wish to explain it, I do not know." It is something like that.

My perspective shifted, that much I can say. I perceived unity, not division, an underlying reality that encompassed all. It was beyond repute, self-evidently true, obviously and undoubtedly the answer to the big riddle. It was a unity that was not juxtaposed to diversity, but encompassed both the One and the many. I felt one with everything, or to be more accurate, there was a oneness of which I was now aware, and in that oneness everything was a part, including myself, and therefore I was one with it.

This merging, this breaking down of the individual barrier, releases a tremendous amount of energy. It brought a blissful feeling, oceanic. It was as if the balloon—what I took for my ego, my I, my me myself—exploded into all of spacetime. It wasn't an explosion exactly. It did not explode. The balloon could not have exploded because in reality there was no balloon. It just vanished. Nothing vanished. Yet it was gone. And it just happened, as if by itself, as I sat in that chair overlooking the street below.

I felt like yelling down to the people passing in the street, "Eureka!" So self-evident, yet so well hidden—right in plain sight. My questions were all gone. And it wasn't as if they were answered. The questions themselves simply vanished. I was left with certainty. Uncommunicable.

It was as if I had touched a high-voltage wire somewhere near the great generating station at the heart of the universe, long before the energy is stepped down for common use, at a voltage that would burn the circuitry of the ordinary man. It opened all my circuits, and my circuitry was changed forever. There was no going back.

The experience was not without its physical expression. I remember that I felt almost weightless, as if my body and everything else was made not of solid matter, but of condensed light. It was as if everything was shimmering. I was buoyant, high as a kite. Though this experience would never wholly leave me, there was a newness to it that made me almost giddy.

After maybe an hour there was a knock at the door. It was a friend of my brother's. He had no idea what had happened to me, and I had no way of expressing it. I didn't even try.

He said, "Let's go out and get some tea." There was a chowk, a crossing in the market, and there was a tea shop.

I thought why not? We can also go for tea. I had no objection. I had no objection to anything anymore. I was entirely at peace, which meant there was a simple acceptance of what was. We were all partaking of a single flow of energy in perpetual movement, a tremendous force which we were all part of.

I understood what Jesus meant by saying, "Not my will, but thine." It is not the will of some personal god, but the universe itself, a single flow moving through us, as if we are all flowing down the same river of water, the River of Life. Though we are making decisions all the time—like to go for tea or not!—even our decisions are not separate from that flow, that underlying place from which everything arises. When the illusion of the balloon disappears, that's what's left. It was just energy passing through us.

We are like drops of water in a mountain stream, each thinking it is separate, each drop believing it is deciding which boulder to flow over, which eddy to enter. What I saw was that we are being pushed from behind, which means that something is already in motion and that we are part of it. Because it contains all, it is unnamable. You can't say it is this or that because it is both this and that. It is *prior* to this and that. It is that from which both this and that arise. Maybe you could call it the matrix. The Taoists call it the Tao, the Way.

Physicists tell us that at the beginning of the universe was the Big Bang, when everything got called into motion. Now it is playing itself out. So if my brother's friend comes and he wants to go out for tea, why not! Let us go. That will also be happening. Tea will be happening!

You can say I jumped levels. As Einstein said, the level of consciousness that creates a problem cannot be used to solve that same problem. Everything was automatically solved. I began to go with the flow.

We went to the tea stall, my brother's friend and me. He ordered two cups of tea. There were two benches and a little wooden table. I wasn't really interested in the tea. I just wanted to sit there. What shimmering vibrance I beheld in the everyday! People were passing through that crossing—on motorcycles, on foot, driving cars, on carts, in rickshaws. And they all looked *so* beautiful. This person on the motorbike, how handsome! That woman crossing the street clutching a bunch of bananas—how graceful. I could not withdraw my eye from anything.

The friend, he was not privy to what I was seeing. He didn't know what had happened, that the world had been transformed. How could he? The poor guy, after some time he must have grown restless with my looking with eyes of wonder over this most common of everyday scenes. I was elder to him, sort of his elder brother, so he couldn't be the one to suggest we leave before I'd drunk my tea, and my tea was untouched. I was hardly aware of him sitting next to me. It was after perhaps an hour, he could take it no longer. He finally said, "Let us go." I thought, why not? Leaving will *also* be happening!

CHAPTER 13

A NEW INTEGRATION

The experience that day turned out to be but a glimpse. What was given was again withdrawn. It took a few days, though it still left me in an elevated state. I did not mind that I was unable to hold onto such clarity. It would be like juggling balls of pure energy. It was inevitable that it would slip through my fingers. Peak experiences are just that. Who hasn't felt some exaltation and its passing? I had been beyond the portals. My doors of perception had opened wide, but the mind is a powerful thing.

The mind separates itself from whatever it encounters, puts it under the lens, and has thoughts about it. It starts passing judgments. It says it is like this, and not like that. It categorizes and draws conclusions. The mind never lets anything just be what it is, in itself. It always has to think about something from which it is separate. It can take a whole and make it many. Every unity divides before its mighty force. It can even take the One and turn it into two. It is that powerful! The mind reduces everything to its own measure. This is an automatic process, based on habits built up over a lifetime.

If you have ever tried to meditate you know you have little or no control over your thoughts. Sit quietly and thoughts will arise in an endless succession, on their own. They are spontaneous. My mind took that blinding clarity and slowly reduced it to the light of common day. It wove its web around it. The mind colonizes whatever it encounters. It clips the wings of vision. In other words, although I was able to grasp the golden ring, I was unable to hold onto it.

Yet something remained. I was no longer the one I was before. I knew now by direct experience that there was but one flow and that we are all part of it. It was that simple, that profound. This fundamental shift of perspective has never left me. Since then, you could say I have had one foot on the other shore, one eye open from the perspective of the One. Yet it was inevitable that the web of thought, the habitual this-and-that mentality, would colonize this central experience and that it would fade in the course of the following days and weeks.

This was because I was not fully cooked. It takes a lifetime to become properly cooked, to ripen, to be ready to leave the pot. At least that's how it was in my case. As I see it, we are all being cooked. At certain points in the alchemical process the elements have to go through the furnace. Matter transforms through increasing levels of energy. Bits are burnt away. What remains is forged anew.

Experience is our furnace. We are here to go through experience, to make mistakes and suffer the natural consequences. As a child, if you fall you skin your knee. Nature's punishment is immediate. And even later in life if you do something stupid, something you should have known better than to have done, it will usually not work out well for you. By nature, a punishment will come. Hindus and Buddhists call it karma. Some monotheists speak of God's justice. Since I am neither religious nor non-religious, I prefer to say nature has a way of balancing itself. It may be the punishment of a bad conscience. It may be literal punishment as meted out by society and lead to a fine or a jail cell. It might make a friend mad. It might even turn a friend into a foe. You might lose money. It might be anything, but things balance out. Missteps come with their counterforce. If you walk into a wall, it will counter your forward motion. It will also hurt.

Until this point I had understood all this, but from a limited perspective. I knew positive actions would be rewarded and no misdeed would ultimately go unpunished. So I was trying in my own way to be good. What I didn't know is that you don't gain much by wrestling with your angels. It is with your demons that you must wrestle. You must lure them into the field, make them manifest, and then fight them.

Until then, I had been trying to act in accordance with that voice inside my head with its ideas of right and good. I was quite

conventional in this respect. I had tried to be good, to act correct-
ly. I had acted in a way that I thought would take me to the light.
Yet what child can learn to walk and to run without skinning his
knee so many times that he learns to be careful? How to grow
without dirtying oneself with experience?

As a youth or even an adult you might fall in love with the
wrong type of person and suffer. You might find yourself in some
other untenable situation. You might do so repeatedly, as we say
unconsciously, until you learn your lesson. The world provides
our lessons for us. You find yourself confronted with a situation.
No matter how difficult it might seem at the time, even when the
road gets rough and you lose your way in some very dark situation, you can say there is a reason you find yourself there. There
are no mistakes. We are here to learn.

Life is forever giving us the chance to learn our lessons. We
might not be conscious enough to take advantage of them. We
may even seem doomed to repeat them. But that doesn't mean
they aren't custom made.

Whatever situation lies before you can be the door to your
awakening. This is what my experience taught me, what was
so liberating, what was left behind by that experience. It might
sound illogical, paradoxical, or like speaking in riddles, but I
would say that on the one hand there are no mistakes; and on the
other, you cannot help but make them. In fact, it is necessary for
your evolution.

CHAPTER 14

INTO THE INFERNO

A few days after this experience I gathered my wife and children and went to my parents' house in order to announce to them all that I had decided to go back to my job. I had been suspended, not fired, so it was not unreasonable to think, if approached in the right manner, that they might take me back. Of course everyone was both surprised and delighted. They'd thought I had finally turned a corner.

For me it was just clearly the path of least resistance. I had a wife and two young children. I was not yet thirty. By trying to stay above the fray and do the 'right thing,' I had only been punished. I'd managed to get myself suspended and in trouble with everyone I knew. I used to want to demand an answer from God, if I could find him, or the universe if I couldn't: Why? Why was I put in a situation in which all the passions and vices were of such easy fulfillment? In the past I had tried to resist, and I judged. I divided the world into what is good and what is bad. Now, I saw, the path ahead was to fulfill those passions that were offered me.

If you don't muddy the waters of experience with your passions you will never move beyond them. You might remain squeaky-clean, but you won't find yourself. The way forward leads right through your demons, your darkness, your passions, your perils. Live your life. Make your mistakes. Take it on at full force!

For better or worse, that was my thinking.

Whatever I've done, I've done with a tremendous amount of energy, with a force greater than that of the common man. I was born like that. When I put my energy to something I usually burn a hole right through it. I go to the excess. Like William Blake once said, "The road to excess leads to the palace of wisdom." It may seem foolish, and I may be a fool, but I always dive into the deepest waters, right where it is most choppy.

That is how I learned wrestling as a youth, and that is what wrestling taught me. Take your opponent like a gift from God. The larger and more powerful the opponent, the more you stand to gain from him, the greater will your strength and cunning be in overcoming him. By wrestling with the forces you encounter, the situations that life presents to you, your muscles grow. By diving into deep water you learn how to become a powerful swimmer.

So take what comes as a sign, as a test and a lesson. If you are religious, you could say a sign from God. If you're not, you could say it is from the universe, based on the laws of nature. Things balance and become unbalanced and thereby all things are matured. Don't you see: we must have both balance and imbalance. These things also arise in mutually dependent pairs. To have something in balance presupposes the existence of imbalance, and vice versa. They arise together.

Nothing is at rest. There is always interaction, movement, and exchanges of energy in everything at all times, from the scale the galaxies and the expanding and contracting universe to the sub-atomic particles. Physicists have even found on the most minute scale—that of the atomic particles, the electrons, photons, and neutrons, and the ever-growing list of subatomic-particles with which they are comprised—that nothing is ever at rest. Nothing is in a static state. The smallest particles are in continual movement and change. They are always vibrating, exchanging energy, you could almost say information, between them.

It is through this exchange that these particles can be detected. It is by a particle's effect on others that they are known. Some physicists even go so far as to say that not only are we only able to detect these smallest of the 'building blocks' of matter by the interactions and effects they have with the particles around them, but that they can only be said to *exist* because of these interactions, and that nothing can be said to exist in isolation. Counterintuitively, relations would then be prior to the individual 'things' being related. This of course begs the question of whether 'things' can be said to exist at all and whether the entire manifest world is really a web, a vast exchange of energy.

It is not that the medieval Roman Church didn't realize everything was in constant flux. It is rather that they cleaved the world in two and banished God to a realm outside the flux. In the medieval Catholic cosmology everything beyond the sphere of the moon was of God and therefore perfect and unchanging or moved in perfect circles. They separated the Unchanging from the Changing. Meanwhile, the Greek philosopher Heraclitus had it right, as far as I'm concerned. He said, *Ta panda rei*, everything flows.

My experience left me with a certainty that not only was everything in continual flux, but that everything is fraught with meaning, you could say. I don't know how to describe it, but from that perspective it was obvious that everything that is happening is happening as part of a seamless whole, and that that whole was in constant flux.

Having been unsuccessful in finding the true and universal scale in which I could weigh my good and bad actions, I realized certain questions to have no answers. The questions themselves must be transcended by a new level of being.

I was now liberated from good and evil. For the first time in my life I felt entirely free to do as I pleased, what the moment called for. I was now a spontaneous man—under none of the normal constraints that people are under, commanded by that voice inside their head telling them what to do and what not to do, which of their desires to fulfill and which not to. I'm sure you know that voice inside your head. Depending on the situation, it might sound like the voice of a policeman, a judge, your nagging mother, a priest, or even your own conscience.

There was no voice any more. No commentary. And it was liberating, being completely and spontaneously free to do anything I wanted. This is not to say I would then go out and commit some act of violence.

Consider the young boy. He is under the force of gravity. He learns to walk. He gets up and he falls, gets up and he falls. Finally he is able to get up and not fall. He has learned how to walk. And though he *could* fall, he does not. He has transcended gravity.

When the boy becomes an adolescent, he comes under the next force, what I call the electromagnetic, with all its attractions and repulsions. This is a tumultuous time. He might have love for this girl and hate that boy who is also liking this girl. One is quick to love; one is quick to hate. These are the passions of youth, the push and pull of emotion.

Then, hopefully, one overcomes this. One reaches the point at which one is at the center of gravity in this force and though one *could* hate, one doesn't. One might not like what another person is doing and that person might even harm you, but you will not hate that person. It will not get to that point. One could then say that you have overcome hate and in so doing you have found your center of gravity in this force. So if I say I had overcome good and evil it doesn't mean that I felt free to now commit despicable acts. I could have. There was no voice stopping me. But I wouldn't.

It is impossible to describe that freedom, what it is like to silence the mind's judgments of each and every thing you encounter. I was liberated, beyond the judgments of good-bad, happy-sad, rich or poor, enlightened or a fool.

Perhaps we are lead to these situations in which we repeatedly find ourselves by our unconscious. But in my thinking, the unconscious is a very large thing; it leads back to the entire universe. Maybe the situations we find ourselves in are woven out of the dreamscape we call the world.

Couldn't the ancient Hindu scriptures have had it right when they said this world is but a dream? They say the god Vishnu is laying upon a twelve-headed serpent floating on the milky ocean of existence and he is dreaming this world into existence. They say we are all figures in his dream. How can we be so certain that this is not true? We cannot. Most would agree with the psychologists who say our nocturnal dreams are full of significance and symbology, that nothing in our dreams is left to chance. Why should 'real life' be so different?

It is as if we all live on a planet under a permanent thick layer of cloud, and that's all we've ever known. Every time we've looked up to the sky, all we've ever seen is this gray. There are rumors that this sky of ours is only a layer of obscuration hiding from our view something wondrous, and that beyond it there is a dark field bright with stars and nebulae and moving planets. They say what we take for the sky, this low layer of gray, is actually a cloud shielding our view.

There are always a few who even say they've seen it themselves, the clouds dispersing to reveal the infinitude beyond. But what if you're not one of them? What can you do? You can either believe what they say or not, perhaps depending on your constitution, and whether you're prone to believing. But you can never be sure. You might long to see what these others claim to have seen. You might join some religion with a whole cosmology. You might read books by people who say they've seen it, and you might speculate on their theories.

Now that I had seen through this obscuring layer of gray, so to speak, I knew. And that could not be taken from me. I had grasped onto the golden ring, and though it had slipped through my fingers, though it was withdrawn, I was a changed man. Some essence remained. There was no turning back. Certain things cannot be taken from you. There are changes to your being.

I began reflecting on my job and my reasons for getting myself suspended. It was mainly because I was resisting what I perceived as the web of corruption my situation was attempting to rope me into. Yet wasn't the truth of the matter that I actually relished the pleasures that would be mine if I gave in and went along with the whole show? Was I really better than the others? Didn't I have lurking within me the same desires, only unfulfilled?

The difference was that I had been born with this damn birthmark on my arm and therefore held myself to a 'higher' standard. Even though an avowed atheist and a communist, wasn't I still striving for that union with something greater, what many call the divine, something that was supposed to be mine by my birthright? What lesson had I to learn in that web of darkness? Was it really to weigh, judge, and resist?

Could it have been placed before me so I could burn through the passions that were lurking within me? Didn't your British poet William Blake once say that those who control their passions do so only because theirs are weak enough to be controlled?

Through the path of controlling my passions I had reached a dead end. But my experience had liberated me from all that. I had no resistance any more. No longer was I looking for a true scale to weigh 'good' and 'bad' actions. I was ready to go back, but this time without restraint. If being the goody-goody had led me to a dead end, how about going the other way?

As a relatively young man in his prime, not yet thirty, I could not quit the field. Even though I had had my experience, I was unable to hold onto it. So now the question arose, born no doubt from my fallen state, but it arose all the same: How to get back to that understanding?

I still had my entanglements, things pushing me forward, compelling me to further mix myself up in the world—children, wife, the whole thing. I had no more resistance to anything. I saw the perfection that was playing itself out.

The experience was still so fresh, it was like riding a wave. I was now much more amenable. I felt no more resistance to anything. Wouldn't returning to my job be the path of least resistance? It would take the pressure off, especially from my family. Then none of them could shake their heads with distain at my throwing away such a high, lucrative, and very important position.

Mustn't we muddy the waters of the innocence that we're born with? We're not here to maintain our innocence; we're here to sully it, to dirty ourselves with the world. We have to temper who and what we are in the fire of experience, and burn away what can be burned off to leave the gold behind.

Who you are when you reach the gold will not be who you are today! That's also what my experience taught me, that human beings are capable of tremendous transformation. We can all see it from the baby to the boy, the boy to the adolescent, and the adolescent to the man. What I'm suggesting here is that there is a further transformation possible, one that completes the circle, that takes us back home.

Although those who have undergone this transformation and have broken through are found in every culture and throughout human history, they are still rare. Yet if you familiarize yourself with their utterances, if you read their writings and listen to their ideas, you will find that they describe their insights in astonishingly similar terms across time and place—exactly as if they are describing various perspectives on the same indescribable something. These utterances were organized and codified by Aldous Huxley in his book *The Perennial Philosophy*, in which he collected the writings of mystics around the world and organized them by common themes.

Mystical insight tends to be described as self-evident—in other words, once experienced, certain things are bloody obvious. There might be no words to describe or explain what you've experienced, but that doesn't necessarily diminish its reality. Imagine describing a sphere to someone living in two dimensions, who only knows circles. A mystic trying to communicate his or her experience is in a similar situation.

Or imagine if, since the beginning, human beings have only seen in black and white. While they might have a rich vocabulary to describe the various shades of grey, there would be no words for colors, no concept even. Now imagine if by some strange fluke, perhaps a knock on the head, you suddenly see the world around you in all its rich colors. Imagine the excitement of suddenly seeing the blue sky, and then, at sunset, instead of seeing it turn to increasingly dark shades of grey, to see it turn red and yellow and pink! Imagine seeing the blush of an apple for the first time, a red rose! What would then happen if you tried to express this excitement. Your tongue would be tied. The truth of colors would be obvious to you, yet how to describe what you see in a world that knows only gradations of grey? What would you say green is, and how does it differ from red? People would think you're nuts! It can be lonely seeing what others don't.

If you live in the world of reason, where everything is questioned and its constituent parts examined, knowledge about which grows with time and is therefore always provisional, if that is your predominant worldview, then you will have a natural antagonism to some ignoramus who comes along and, without producing any evidence other than his own immediate experiential knowing, says his truth is self-evident and therefore absolute.

Don't you see? There it is again, the question of science and intuition, the question of the parts to the whole and whether one can know the whole through its parts. With intuition, knowledge doesn't come in bits and pieces, but as a ready whole. Reason knows only ratio, the relation of the one with the other. Reason takes whatever it finds whole and divides it into its constituent parts and gains knowledge by the relations between them.

This is all very good when building bridges and dams. But what if there really were another kind of knowledge, another way of knowing, as the mystics have claimed from the beginning? Here in India we say, especially when counseling the young, "No knowledge without college." But to what type of knowledge does that refer? It refers to the type of knowledge that can be built up over time and can be taught and must be learned. Yes, a Master's degree brings with it an increase of knowledge on your given subject, and a PhD even more than that.

I'll tell you a secret, an open secret, which if you want you can put into your book: there is a kind of knowledge that is not made up of parts, but is whole. It is beyond words to describe. You cannot piece it together to learn it. You cannot reduce it to its parts to understand it. It can be learned no more than it can be taught. Yet it can be experienced, and once experienced it cannot be doubted. While it is possible to doubt an opinion or a belief, experience takes us to another level, beyond the dichotomy of belief and doubt. Is it possible to doubt the taste of salt? Need one have faith in it? When you experience something, you know it.

The whole will always elude the reasoned thinker. You cannot add things together to reach the whole. The whole, being whole, is whole. If you break it into pieces, it is no longer whole. It is that simple. Maybe I shouldn't say this too loud, not in this day and age, but I suppose they no longer burn heretics at the stake: by taking things apart and comparing them you will never reach the whole.

Let me give you an example of how science as it is presently conducted will never arrive at an understanding of the One, and will never reach their coveted Unified Theory of Everything. Let's say someone loans money to a friend, who says he will pay off half the debt after one week and half of what's left after two weeks, and half of that the next. Don't you see? He'll never pay it all back. It will never end! Half, half, half, half—and you'll never reach the whole. This is science, stuck like Zeno in his paradox.

The rational mind is extremely good at dividing reality, but like Humpty Dumpty is unable to put the egg back to rights. The apprehension of the universe on a more fundamental level, taking into account the One and its relation to the many, entails a kind of knowing that cannot be put into numbers and equations.

If you take an animal and dissect it, you may know your anatomy and be able to sew it back together again in the proper order, but you can never give back the life taken by your knife.

When we're talking about entangling ourselves in the world, what we're really talking about is what is personified in Hindu thinking as the endless play of the god Shiva and his consort Parvati, energy and form. Energy must become entangled in form, in matter, in order to transform. A beam of light is pure energy. If it is passing through the vacuum of interstellar space encountering not a single atom of matter it would continue unchanged forever, never manifesting as light as we know it.

In fact, interstellar space, though shot through with beams of light originating in every star out there, is jet black. This is because that space is empty, it contains no matter. Until the beam of light encounters matter, it is darkness itself. It is only when light strikes matter that it illuminates—only then is it capable of firing the neurons in our eyes. It is the same if you hold a flashlight over your head and shine it straight up into the night sky. You will not even know if it is on or off unless there is smoke or fog in the air. Only then will you see the cone of light.

Say you're floating in space, interplanetary space, empty space, space with no atoms of matter floating through it. It is jet black all around you. It is empty. There is nothing there. You look out, and between the distant stars it is as black as inside the deepest cave on earth. Though shot through with light, it is devoid of light. Though light is passing through the space before you, it strikes nothing, and therefore there is not one photon to strike the retina of your eye. You see the points of light of distant stars, but they are set in a field of total blackness. There is no atmosphere as there is on Earth to scatter the light, so the blackness between these points of light is profound and complete. And that blackness of space between the stars is just as dark as the space between your outstretched hands. If there is no matter, nothing for it to strike, light is really blackness itself, pure and unadulterated. Pure energy unencumbered by matter.

Now let's say you float an orange in the space before you at an arms' length. See it brilliantly shining in the light of the sun that's been passing through this space the whole time.

The point is that though intense sunlight is passing through the square of space before you, there is no light. It is the same blackness of interstellar space—until you place some matter there. Then the energy interacts with the matter and light is produced, you could say, made manifest—however you want to call it.

Light manifests—it becomes light—by entangling with matter. It is by encountering matter and scattering photons of light that we can 'see' it. This is an example of how energy transforms through its entanglement with matter. Darkness is turned to light! Energy takes form. A wave becomes a particle, in this case a photon of light. Energy needs matter to transform no less than matter needs energy to be transformed. In India, this is what we call the endless play of Shiva and Parvati.

It is rather like the shells of electrons the scientists speak of. By adding energy to the atomic system, an electron jumps to the next level, the next orbit, what they call the next shell. And they tell us the electron doesn't move from one shell to the next. It is never half-way to the next shell. It is as if the earth were to widen its orbit from its present orbit to that of the next planet out, Mars, without passing through the intervening space, but by simply appearing in the wider orbit, instantly. It jumps from one state to another; it makes a quantum jump. This is how human transformation occurs as well.

CHAPTER 15

REINSTATEMENT

When I announced that I'd get myself reinstated to my job, my family insisted on bringing me to a village doctor. Since I had no more resistance to anything, I agreed. The doctor provided some Ayurvedic medicine, maybe some herbs. I took them just to please my wife and my parents and everyone around, even though I knew my experience had cured me of almost everything—both in my body and in my mind. My jaundice disappeared, and I regained my strength.

I've always known that my physical ailments have their roots elsewhere. Like this heart I walk around with, surrounded by blood vessels that every doctor who has looked into it in the last years has insisted are in need of immediate repair. They always speak of emergency bypass surgery. Yet I've never let them take a knife to me. To cure a thing, first you must know its true cause. Without that, none of their medicine would benefit. One said it's a miracle I'm even alive. I have no problem living with uncertainty. It sharpens the senses.

A few days after I announced that I would go back to the job, I went to the official in Chandigarh who would be responsible for my reinstatement. He knew the story of my suspension and that I could be trouble. But he also knew that when in the mood I could do triple the work of any other SDO, Sub-Divisional Officer, and that he could count on more projects in my district. Since every project had its contracts and kickbacks, which were worked up the line, this would be good for him. It is why he would be willing to take a chance on me. And besides, my belligerence had given way to a feeling of peace with whatever was happening, no matter what it was. It must have shown. I must have appeared

90

before him a changed man. Still, since I was asking him to take a gamble on me, it was natural that he would want something for it, something up front. This was clear even before I entered his office. In other words it would involve a bribe.

Paying a bribe seemed a fitting entrance into my new life exploring the darker regions. You could call it my toll tax on my own personal road to hell. We need not go into detail of how much money I gave, but an exchange of money was involved. Usually these things are done in a discrete manner, through intermediaries. But this time the official himself came right out point blank and told me how much it would cost me, and it was a huge sum. I didn't have that kind of money. My wife was ready to sell all her gold. But I said no.

Somehow, I got some money. I don't really recall how I got it, but maybe I got it from my mother. Or maybe my wife had some with her. Wives usually keep some money apart from what their husbands know. Maybe they each gave me some. I went back and paid the official half of what he was asking and promised to pay the rest after joining the service. By the time I walked out of his office, I was given papers for a new job.

Again, I had a bungalow and a car and driver and all the perks. I brought my wife and children to my new posting and we began our new life there.

I had been given a large but out-of-the-way district that hadn't had a senior officer for some time. So there were no projects underway and not much work. Because of this, I was free—free to let loose and do as I pleased.

I became immediate friends with my second-in-command. There was really nothing for us to do. So we'd have our driver take us to a restaurant to pass time. We ate, we drank, we played cards—and we gambled. In the meantime work began to come.

Now that I wasn't wasting my energy on useless questions and on being belligerent, I could apply my prodigious energy more effectively to the work at hand, which seemed to get done effortlessly, no matter what it was. This was noticed by my superiors, and more work came. Soon I was overseeing large projects throughout my district. The money was rolling in, and I was living like a king.

In some respects my experience faded—it *was* a peak experience with maximum clarity. But in other respects it has never diminished. It cannot. If an experience is true and goes deep enough, it will be with you forever. It is not a collection of new facts about the world or an idea that can be learned and then forgotten. It is an experience, and once experienced, a thing is known. There is nothing left to be either believed in or doubted.

I had made a quantum jump, not one in degree, but in kind. I had been rewired. The change was not horizontal, but vertical. And there are paradoxes between such vertical shifts of perspective, as if you have to dive off one shore and swim to another, passing through some fluid element in-between. The solid earth of your understanding must dissolve before the new land can emerge out of the waters.

This shift of perspective called into question some of our most basic notions of how the cosmos operates, things so fundamental that to even question them would seem either foolish or mad.

What am I talking about? I realized, for instance, that when somebody is doing something, say, lifting a pencil, nobody is lifting a pencil. Pencil lifting is happening, but actually there is nobody there to raise the pencil. It was the crazy realization that nobody is doing anything! Things are happening, but that there is a separate individual doing this or that was experienced to be an illusion.

This is not an intellectual thing; you cannot learn to see it this way. It is a matter of experience. And as I said, once a thing is experienced, it is known. The very notion of the individual, the ego, the sense of I as an entity that can do or act, was blown out of the water! If someone tells you the goal of the spiritual path is to get rid of the ego, I'd say they still do not understand—because the whole point is that there is no ego to get rid of. It is that simple!

This might not make sense to you; it might even sound crazy. Yet everybody who has read the Hindus' most sacred book, the Bhagavad Gita, knows that one of its essential teachings is that 'you are not the doer.' This was also a central teaching of that great 20th century Indian sage, Ramana Maharshi. It is a core tenet of Eastern thought and has been for thousands of years. Yet what does it mean? Is it a riddle? One reads it, one hears the sages say it, over and over in any number of enigmatic ways: "Things happen, deeds are done, but there is no individual doer thereof." On the surface, and by common reckoning, it makes no sense. Yet from this other perspective, this enigmatic and even incomprehensible notion is bloody obvious, self-evident in fact. As I said before, just try explaining to someone living in two dimensions what a sphere is. Good luck!

And so it was comical, especially at the beginning, when I first restarted my job, to see everyone running around so earnestly, jockeying for position, as if they were doing this and doing that, while to me it was obvious that everything was just happening, like those bubbles on a stream bumping into each other and flowing over boulders and getting caught in little eddies, all driven by the single flow.

Even though everyone was acting as if they were trying to take advantage of this and that situation in the name of gaining money and enjoying, I saw that it was all just a big play. It was both comical and at times tragic to see it thus, and yet it was always freeing. I never felt happier. Since people would have thought me mad, I could speak of it with no one. It was like my own private joke.

Who, these days, these rationally minded days, would ever put up with substituting paradox for fact? Open your mouth about certain subjects and you will find yourself making indefensible statements entirely at odds with common sense. It will only cause confusion.

Imagine finding yourself on a stage, acting in a play, and suddenly realizing that the other actors are playing their parts with such sincerity that they have fallen into a trance. They are identifying so completely with their parts that they no longer remember that they are only actors acting. Without putting too fine a point on it, that is what it was like. I, too, had been in that trance, and realized it only the moment I woke up. This didn't free me from having to act my part. There was no question of my leaving the stage. I was still a husband, a father, and, once again, a Sub-Divisional Officer. Nothing changed that. In fact, if anything, I played my part with greater energy and passion than

I had before, now that I wasn't wasting so much energy in that
trance-like state most call normal waking reality.

Words have not been created to express this experience. It
would be laughable to even try. The Understanding flies in the
face of everything we know. Only if you've ever had a glimpse of
this one flow will you know what I mean. Many people have had
a glimmer. That's what sets off that longing; that's often what
turns people into 'spiritual seekers,' who are often the most comical of all, thinking they have to *do* something in order to reach
the Understanding!

Enough said.

The point is that I was now free floating, like a cloud, shifting with the wind. If we watch a cloud skirting across the sky, it
is clear the cloud has no real say in which way it goes: it is going this way and that at the behest of the wind, an invisible yet
powerful force. Wind brings both sun and rain. It can make a leaf
flutter; it can blow a roof off a house. Yet have you ever *seen* the
wind? No! You have only seen its effects. We find nothing extraordinary when even the trunk of a mighty oak is being swayed by
an invisible force.

The way people were running around as if they were deciding
to do this or that was as ludicrous to me as it would have been if a
cloud, for our purposes here a conscious being, were to forget the
very concept of wind and get the crazy notion that *it* was deciding
which way to go. Naturally, the cloud would come up with justi-
fications for why it decided to head north—just when the wind
happened to swing in that direction.

How to describe this shift of perspective without sounding like
a holy fool? Am I saying we have no free will? What words can
one use to express the tremendous release that comes with the
realization that we are being blown from behind. Another way of
saying it would be that we are all part and parcel of something
infinitely greater than our individual selves, the awareness of
which comes with a tremendous release.

A famous ancient Hindu formula expresses exactly this: *Sat,
Chit, Ananda*—Being, Awareness, Bliss. Being, or Truth, is already there, underlying, whether we know it or not. Then comes
the *awareness* of this already-existing underlying reality. And

with this awareness comes bliss, a release. It is really quite simple. Indian philosophers have been speaking of this for more than two and a half thousand years. And though the sages of old proclaimed it as the deepest truth, how to express the lived reality of this, today, in this day and age, without sounding like a fool?

Another way of seeing it would perhaps be that I was shifting because of my desires, and at that time I indulged in every one of them. I worked hard, but work was easy for me: I had so much energy that I could outperform them all. I enjoyed myself to the hilt! That would be one way of seeing it.

But really all that was happening was due to the people and the situations surrounding me. If somebody said, Let's do this. Let's enjoy going there. Let's go to Shimla, I would simply go along. My junior engineers, or some friend, another SDO, or some contractor, or some two, three others, they would say, "Let us have a party today. Let us enjoy drink and see who we might meet along the way." I'd go along. I was just a witness to things.

This birthmark has never left my arm; its imprint on my life has been just as enduring. This baba thing has been both my blessing and sparring partner since the beginning. Never has its effect on my life not been there, one way or the other. With the same fervor and energy that previously I had directed towards trying to *be* the baba, I now applied to trying to *kill* the baba. I went into open rebellion. Whatever a baba was supposed to do, I did exactly the opposite. I had already become an atheist and then a communist. Now I drank, I smoked, I did this and that, things I won't even mention.

My wife noticed what was happening and asked why I was going to such the other extreme. This is what I told her: "I am like an arrow strung on a bow, pulled back in the direction of baba-hood. What do you expect to happen when it is released? It will *have to* fly to the opposite extreme."

If under normal circumstances I might have taken two drinks—now I took the whole bottle! Pure rebellion. I was realizing my freedom. I am. I am free. Things were happening around and through me. I won't mention all I did during this period of my life, but you can say I did everything. I went to the other extreme.

Buddhists talk of the Middle Way, that way of moderation between self-indulgence of sensory pleasure on the one hand, and the saintly abstention of desire on the other. What rubbish, I thought! Bunch of pious nonsense! How can I know *my* middle way if I don't test the extremes, if I don't *experience* them? Remember what Carl Jung said about the inferno of the passions? If you don't pass through your passions, if you don't experience them, you'll never overcome them. They will remain lurking there in the background, dogging at your heals, and they will not let you be.

Many who follow the Buddha's Middle Way actually have these thoughts, these desires, these passions lurking within, but they never live them. They stick to their Middle Way and they hide these thoughts, these desires that refuse to conform. They hide these things even from themselves, these never fulfilled passions, and they never go away. They never evolve beyond them. They don't muddy themselves in experience, all the while thinking they are so pure. This, I believe, is a mistake. In all the things I did, I felt there was nothing to be ashamed of. I was free of all that!

I would neither say no, nor yes, to anything. I would not go to my senior for more work, even though more work would mean earning more money. I would neither refuse nor ask for work. And when he brought me a new project he would ask, "In how many days can you complete this work?" I would tell him, "No, you tell me. I can execute this work in however many days you want. Tell me how many days any other man would take, and I will do it in half."

I had the power to execute work in any amount of time. No problem. Whatever work they gave me, they knew it was as good as done.

Nothing was impossible for me. I felt like a 1,000-watt bulb!

My friends in the department called me the Steamroller. I did have a fleet of steamrollers under my command. But that's not why they called me that. They used to joke that I was a steamroller—a steamroller being used to press clothes!

One time an old man, a poor farmer, came to my office. He needed a culvert built under the road because the water was backing up and flooding his fields. He'd been trying for the past two or three years. Because of the nature of the project, there were two departments involved, one that controls water courses and the other that makes roads and culverts. He had been bounced between the two departments for years, each throwing up impediments. Actually they were just trying to extract money out of the poor man.

I grasped the situation at once and told the man not to worry. "When you pass down that road tomorrow morning the culvert will be built." This was obviously an absurd thing to say, since the Public Works Department would normally take weeks or even months once a project was approved just to complete the paperwork. Even though he thought I was ridiculing him, the old man didn't want to antagonize. He put on an obsequious smile and stood. As he left my office, I called out to him, "Just look tomorrow."

I gathered my crew and told them there'd be no sleep that night, and they set to work.

The next morning the culvert was in place. To the finish! I had told my subordinates to leave not a trace of the construction, to smooth the earth down and clean up the pans where the bitumen was heated, everything. The only difference should be that a culvert was there.

Another time, it was suddenly announced that Prime Minister Rajiv Gandhi was to come to where I was posted for a big public function. When the prime minister comes to some state, the entire state government comes out. There are school groups, military bands, and thousands of people. A huge stage must be constructed. Arrangements must be made for so many tens of thousands of people. Usually, there are months of advance notice. This time it was very sudden. The prime minister was arriving in two days' time, and the stage had to be completed by tomorrow night.

My boss, knowing my record, asked me to be responsible for the stage.

I said, OK. He knew if I said I'd do it, the work was as good as done. I told my wife, "You will not see me in the next days." I called all my junior engineers, contractors, even the clerical staff. We were a team. They would die for me, sort of. They all left their homes also.

I prepared a plan with lists of materials needed and who would do what. I gave instructions to each of them, down to the utmost detail, what to do if this or that happens.

I told them, "You will not come to me and say I cannot complete my task. I am not bothered about the means, only about the ends. I am bothered about the job being done. Whatever it takes, take it—and get it done."

No one would have dared say, "I couldn't do it." My eyes would have killed them! Either the work is done, or it is not done. All else is mere excuses. I could even accept if they said from the start that they couldn't do it. Even saying no from the start was acceptable to me, rather than giving excuses later on.

I told them excuses come into the picture only when you are not fully prepared from your soul. If you come to me and say you couldn't do it because the rain came, I'd say, "The rain couldn't have come if you had willed it strongly enough. You were not prepared. You were not into it enough from your soul! Don't tell me rain happened. Nothing will happen if your soul is prepared."

And it's true: if you put your soul into it, you can do anything.

So I put my plan into action. Everybody had their part, and I could kick back and watch it roll.

The next day my superior came to check up on me. His neck was on the line if anything went wrong with the prime minister's visit. He walked into my office and I was sitting, leaning back with my legs up on my desk. I think I was dozing.

He was furious. "The prime minister is coming tomorrow morning, you fool! I made you responsible. And you're just sitting there?"

What he didn't understand was that some work is practically invisible to the eye. Everybody can see physical work. A road gets constructed, a building goes up. But other work—mental work, intellectual work—is not so readily seen; it is seen only by others who do such kind of work.

Actually, the deeper the work the less visible it is. That is why hardly anyone sees God's work. God, or the forces, the Tao, whatever you want to call it—or even better call it nothing at all. Hardly anybody sees God's work. But if you go deep enough, you will not miss it. You will see. Rather you will see it is *all* the working of that Super Force, what people call God.

Anyway, my superior came and was furious to see me sitting idly when the prime minister was due in less than twelve hours. I told him to go out to the site and have a look. He did, and saw that all was well. My workers were putting the final touches on the stage.

Chapter 16

Eight Year Descent

For the next eight years you can say I made my descent into Hades. Directed by my passions, a darkness lead me forward. The light path had gotten me nowhere and left me stranded, so I went the other way. At the time, I didn't know where I was going or why. It was only later that I read C. G. Jung's autobiography where he expounded upon the importance of passing through darkness, manifesting and wrestling your demons. It was only later that I heard about the 'Lefthand Path' of the tantrics, the *vamachara*. In the Lefthand Path, one breaks all the taboos of polite society in order to release the energy that is pent up there. And in retrospect, I can see that that is exactly what I was doing. I broke every rule and enjoyed life to the hilt—even though there was nobody there to enjoy it! Things were just happening—that was how I experienced it. Instead of an I, an ego, at the center of my existence, there was a big empty space.

Now I can see what I wanted, without really realizing it, was to get rid of this body and this mind—to burn it all through and leave behind an empty shell. You could say I was becoming disorganized in preparation for organizing around a new I, a new body even. Disintegrating in order to reintegrate.

I was still intermittently high as a kite, having glimpses beyond the separation of individuality to the unity beyond. But it is also true that I was dying. I was like a rock, falling on its own, weightless, sometimes giddy as it plummeted.

Doesn't a seed have to wither away fully and be buried in order to give birth to a new plant? Isn't that what it is to be reborn? My previous self was dying. People think resurrection is to literally die and be reborn. I don't see it that way. You are still reborn, you resurrect, but it is in another way. Your body continues, but something inside your mind and body has changed, has taken a new turn. You are reborn into something, in some different way. It is to die while living.

In my first experience you could say I had a glimpse. But it was taken away. That is because I wasn't ready. The key slipped through my hands. The gates closed. I couldn't find my way back. Imagine if the oxygen was withdrawn from the air you breathed. Now you can imagine the panic I was in. What was the purpose of all this struggle if there was no road back to that oneness? It was like a riddle. You could even say I knew the answer to the riddle, but it no longer made sense! I had the key. It was the right key; it had worked before, but the door still wouldn't open. It was agony. What else was life worth living for? Was it enough to be like that balloon that one day will pop? And thus I came to that crossroads—what I call the crossroads of my life. But it felt more like a dead end.

I started doing every wrong thing, everything that is not permitted by society. Like smoking. That is especially taboo in our religion. I also made money, enjoyed myself, drank. I did everything else. We needn't go into it here, but perhaps you can imagine. Actually I did not know what was happening. I hadn't a clue how to orient myself. Yet functioned at my job. I got my work done. You cannot imagine the energy I had, what kind of power was released after that experience. Nothing was impossible for me. I had that much power. One must have that much energy, that much power. There was no I in myself. I was just free. There was no purpose.

You may well ask, "Did you do corruption?" But that might not be the best word to describe it. So if you write my story, please don't use that word. The right way of saying it would be that having been freed of the persona of saint, and having realized my freedom, I did what was before me. And because I had more energy than other people, I went to the other extreme. So you should not say I did corruption. You can say I did to the extreme what everybody else was doing to their limited capacity! This is the right way of saying it. I was doing everything while at the same time doing nothing. The eye of the storm. It is up to you how to write that.

There was always a difference between the others and me, since to me things just seemed to be happening on their own. It was as if I had been thrown from a cliff. Led by my desires, I was moving on my own to the bottom. There was no purpose. Nothing. In retrospect I can see that the purpose was to cleanse myself of all worldly desires.

It's like this: let's say I had lots of money—then I would not have to bother about it. The desire for money would not remain in my mind. By having a desire and fulfilling it, I was emptying myself of that desire. I was emptying myself of all the usual human needs. The Buddha said desire is the cause of suffering, and I was not without my share. It was as if my soul, the ground, the core of my being, knew that to get to the next destination first I had to get rid of the present mind/body. What I felt was something like I was going to my death. That is why I smoked and drank so much. Neither before nor after have I forgotten my body to such an extent, nor taken so little care of it.

This went on for some seven or eight years, by the end of which I lost interest in the job and all the pleasures it brought me. So I simply stopped going in to work. It took some time, but when they realized I had really stopped appearing at my office they posted somebody else in my place. They neither suspended me, nor not suspended me. I was certainly not fired. Actually nothing happened. They just posted somebody in my place, neither provisionally nor permanently.

Having fulfilled my desires, having emptied myself of them, they had no power over me. Whatever I had wanted to do, I had done it. I had gotten some money. I had enjoyed life. I drank. I had done everything. I had finished this thing. Emptied myself. Even if I had wanted to, I could no longer enjoy myself in that way—I just could not.

And so it was that I was done with the job. It was not easy. The whole world was harassing me. "Why are you sitting at home?

Not many people can become an engineer. Such a good job, and you are leaving it—for what? For nothing!"

It was worse than the first time, when I had gotten myself suspended for fighting with the officer. This time I had just stopped going. It was tantamount to quitting, but had none of the finality of a decisive step. I just simply started staying home. The first time, when I was suspended, I still had the power of youth and the robust body of a wrestler. Now I was spent, a mere shell, ruined by the life I had led, the drink, the smoke. I was overweight and sickly.

My parents and in-laws again began worrying for their grandchildren. Friends and relatives tried to intervene. Everybody wanted to get involved in righting me, convincing me not to give up such a promising future. They told me not to think only of myself, but of the wellbeing of my family. They warned me not to throw my life away.

But there were two forces at war. One came from without, this endless needling of family, friends, and colleagues, none of whom could possibly understand that there was another force that they could neither see nor imagine, a dark force that was far less defined. A strong unconscious hand. Something that would not let me out of its grip. It had me acting in ways counter to all common sense.

Now I can see it in context. I've studied enough the experiences of others who have gone through spiritual awakenings to see that it often entails a dissolution—a Dark Night of the Soul, such as that experienced by St. Theresa of Avila and St. John of the Cross. It is as if the awakening comes in these cases as a war between the primal powers of the light and the dark.

Looking back, I can see that is what I was going through. But at the time it felt like my raft had plunged over a waterfall and was yet to hit bottom. Once set in motion, there was no stopping it. Because I could not understand what was happening to me, I could not control it. There was no question of my returning to the life of a public works engineer. It was like a force of gravity, sucking me inexorably down the rabbit hole into myself. I was at war with myself and the world.

CHAPTER 17

THE ACCIDENT

In such a double-bind I met with an accident. I easily could have died.

What happened was this: as I told you, I just stopped going to my office. I didn't tell anybody I would not be coming. I made no excuses. I just simply ceased going. My subordinates, my junior engineers, sub engineers, my entire crew covered for me as long as possible. My superiors knew I had absconded, or rather had just quietly disappeared, but they didn't know what to do with me. They had never had a case like mine. I was neither here nor there—neither fired nor suspended nor had I quit the job. It was like everything else in my life at that time: I was somewhere in-between, neither this nor that.

Everybody was trying to compel me—my wife, her family, my parents—but they couldn't. Maybe it was because of my hearing, but I felt as if I just could not understand what they were saying.

Then, one day—it must have been after six or seven months of my sitting idly, neither wanting to do the job nor knowing what I was supposed to do in lieu of it—a few of my junior engineers came to my house. They told me my superiors had decided I was never coming back and were about to appoint someone else to permanently occupy my chair.

They said it was quickly reaching the point at which if I ever bothered to come back they would fire me.

My team, they loved me and didn't want to work under anyone else. We got our work done, but we didn't play by the rules. Ever since my experience, I didn't give a damn for amassing more only for myself. So those working under me did exceptionally well. Since we had enjoyed together, we were also friends.

They desperately wanted me back.

One of my junior engineers, he had been with me the longest, spoke up.

"Maybe you feel shy going back and asking to be reinstated," he said, "but I can help you. I will do everything. My friend is a big politician, an MLA, a Member of the Legislative Assembly. I've told him about you, and he is waiting. All you have to do is go with me to see him. I will do all the talking. He's my friend and he will get you reinstated."

My wife was in the room. It seemed they had already spoken to her about it. It could have been a conspiracy. She was saying how pleased both her parents and mine would be by the news that I was ready to stop this nonsense and return to my professional life. My subordinates were all agreeing. It turned out that the MLA, having already been told about my case, was expecting me later that day in Chandigarh. He was a powerful MLA. I could not refuse.

My subordinate packed me into his car and drove me to Chandigarh, where we met the MLA. But before we had time to discuss my case, the MLA said he had to leave right then for Shimla for a party meeting—or maybe it was just to go to a party. It was never quite clear. But he was a busy man, and we could discuss my case on the way. He said that in the morning, after we'd returned to Chandigarh, he could get me my orders. This is how politicians work, completing their own work while doing work for others. There are always hidden motives, winks, and nods. The MLA's driver drove up in one of those solid, plush luxury vehicles with tinted windows that politicians drive around in. We all got in and we set off for Shimla. This is normally a journey of three or four hours. It was on the way that I met with that accident.

The MLA, it turned out, was something of an alcoholic. He pulled out a bottle of whisky as soon as we set off. My junior engineer was a drinker too. I was not into it at that time. I had lost interest in everything—drinking, smoking—everything I did while on the job. But I was with them. So I also drank, and we moved from Chandigarh towards Shimla.

At about ten thirty at night we were all becoming hungry and had to pee. So we stopped at one of those hotel/restaurants found

on the side of major roads that are run by the State Tourism Department. We sat at a table outside on the lawns and first we
ordered a bottle of whiskey, some soda, and a bucket of ice. With
time, quite naturally, we all became quite drunk.

We became hungry too, so we decided to order some dinner.
My junior engineer called out to the waiter and told him of our
desire. But it was well past eleven by now. The waiter said the
restaurant was closed and they were taking no more orders.

The junior engineer, he was also a bit mad! He lifted himself
hastily—if unsteadily—out of his chair and started yelling, his
speech slurred from drink, "You have to serve us. Do you know
who this is? He is a member of the Legislative Assembly! This
restaurant is run by the State Tourism Department; therefore,
he is your boss! You cannot possibly refuse him dinner. How dare
you? Open your kitchen at once!"

The waiter stood his ground. Voices were raised, and it was
getting hotter and hotter. From my own side, I was still in that
state of acceptance, realizing it was all part of that one big flow.
I sat there, somewhat intoxicated, watching, taking no side, and
with no particular compulsion to get involved. The only time I
opened my mouth was to tell the hotel wallah that he might as
well realize that he would have to serve us dinner sooner or later because the MLA was there. For me it was a practical piece of
advice, a matter of fact.

As will happen in India when men begin to argue and a
fight seems likely, a crowd of twenty or thirty people quickly gathered in a circle around us. The entire hotel staff, the
waiters, the guests from the hotel who had heard the argument
brewing—everybody was there, even the manager, who came
pushing through the crowd. The situation was, to say the least,
becoming fluid.

The junior engineer made one too many sassy remarks to the
manager, such that his underlings felt obliged to protect his hon-
or, and they pushed my subordinate to the ground and began
kicking him mercilessly.

Slowly rising from my chair, I started edging away. The MLA
also got up, but no one would dare touch him. Still, he was pushed
two or three times. They let him leave the circle, I thought maybe

to go to the car and get his pistol, which I knew he kept there. Or maybe he was going inside to call for help.

Within a short time, I could feel the mob growing bored with beating the engineer, especially since he had stopped responding. He must have been in shock. With the MLA gone, it was pretty easy to guess their unsatiated anger would now shift towards me—even though I hadn't abused anyone. I had merely offered them that one bit of friendly advice, that since he really was an MLA, in the end they'd have to provide food, so they might just as well do it. But I, too, had been drinking. My tone could have been just a bit sharp. So I guessed I was next in line to be taught a lesson.

I was terrified of getting such a beating. I would have been less afraid if I was going to be shot. But to be beat by a crowd with their fists and their feet, to be the object of their blood anger... I got panicky and began looking for which way to run. The hotel was above the road, set back atop a series of wide terraces. We were on one lawn. Some twenty feet below, there was another lawn. And about twenty feet below that was yet another. Then there was the road.

Without anyone quite noticing, I maneuvered myself to the edge of where the land dropped off to the next terrace. A tree grew down there that almost reached the level we were on. If I jumped, I could catch hold of a branch. No doubt it would snap, and everybody would realize I was trying to escape. But it would hopefully break my fall.

So when I saw them growing bored with beating the junior engineer, I just sort of moved a couple of steps over, and I jumped. I caught hold of a branch as planned. The branch broke and I fell on the ground.

Luckily, I landed on my feet. But unluckily there was an iron pipe coming straight out of the ground, raised five or six inches, and my right heel landed directly onto it. Here, you can see it. After thirty, forty years, it is still permanently swollen and misshaped.

My Achilles' got broken. The bone was looking out.

Even if they had overlooked the sound of the breaking branch, they never could have missed my scream of agony, the animal cry of pain that issued from between my lips. Above me I could hear voices calling out, "Catch him! Catch him!"

With a potent mix of adrenaline and alcohol coursing through my bloodstream, I somehow jumped to the next terrace. They came from the other side to cut me off. With that broken heel and the bone sticking out I had to run across that terraced lawn. Now that I had been caught trying to escape, they would surely try to kill me. Then I had to jump again, this time to the paved road, which was busy with traffic and little tea and vegetable stalls, where I thought I'd be safe from the mob. I was in such a panic that I jumped, putting my weight on the other leg while landing.

Anything could have happened at that moment. A good dozen of them had broken off from where they were beating the junior engineer, and they came running down the road. Leading the way was the restaurant watchman with his wooden rod in his hand, the type wielded by low-level security guards across India. We call them *lathis*. It was maybe four or five feet long. He came right at me, raised the *lathi* high above his head, and struck me square on the skull. Blood gushed down my face and started soaking into my clothes.

Surely, I was done for.

Just as the watchman was about to strike me again something happened. I can't really say how, but I got an inspiration. It probably saved my life. Before I knew what I was doing—this was the split second before the rod was to be used again—I called out: "Only that person should come forward to strike me to whom I have said anything."

There must have been something in the way I said it, the calm with which I spoke. Like Christ saying, "Who amongst you shall throw the first stone?" Everybody stopped dead in their tracks, almost frozen. Even the rod wallah. Perhaps some power came through me. Something that could not be stopped. Or maybe they were just scared, not only seeing all the blood gushing from my head but also my foot with the bone sticking out. Maybe they were afraid I might die. For whatever reason, nobody touched me.

Rather, one man lifted me under one arm and another man lifted me by the other and they half-carried, half-dragged me back up to the hotel. Some even began to sympathize with me, defending me against those who had stayed behind and wanted to do to me what they had done to the junior engineer. They took me to the restaurant and sat me on a bench outside. They were done beating the junior engineer and he was now sitting on a chair, bruised but looking remarkably intact. Two policemen had come in the meantime. Perhaps the MLA had phoned them.

The manager brought me a bottle of whisky, which I gulped greedily to cover the pain. It was my only hope, to be so drunk that I wouldn't feel the fractured bone that had pierced the skin of my ankle. After ten or fifteen minutes the MLA and the police wallah reached a settlement. They came to where I lay on the bench—the MLA, my junior engineer, and our driver. "Let us go," they said. "This thing is finished."

They lifted me and brought me to the car. When we reached the main road below the hotel, the MLA said, "Let us go back to Chandigarh. I am not in the mood for Shimla."

The blood had dried on my forehead, and my heel had also stopped bleeding. In fact, it had turned white. I remember wondering where all the blood went. Even though the bone was sticking out, I said, and I must have been really drunk, "No. Men don't turn back from what they set out to do, not with such minor problems! We will go as planned. We will go to Shimla, you will do your work there, and tomorrow we shall come back." I must have said it forcefully—and they must also still have been drunk—for they agreed.

When we arrived at the outskirts of Shimla, we got rooms in the first hotel we saw. After two or three hours, when the whiskey had finished off from inside my body, I came to unbearable pain. I had not been aware of this pain, but there it was, and it was excruciating. My junior engineer brought a doctor who said there was nothing he could do but give me pain killers and sedatives. In the morning, he said, we should go to Chandigarh where there was a hospital that could handle such cases.

Despite the sedative, I spent the night in incredible pain. I couldn't go by myself to the toilet, even for passing urine. And I had drunk so much that my bladder kept filling. My junior engineer had to take me there. But how many times could I wake him up to go with me? So in the end I had to crawl on my knees.

In the morning we went back to the Punjab and I had them drop me off at my home. We had decided not to tell anyone what had really happened. We would just say that we met with an accident.

Those days, in the village, we were not quick to rush to a doctor. There were some things we could do at home, natural remedies, and I stayed home for ten days. And then my brother-in-law came—the husband of my wife's sister. He's a doctor. They must have summoned him. He came and examined my heel. He said the whole of this heel was fractured inside and if I didn't get it operated on immediately they may have to cut off the entire foot. So I allowed him to take me to the hospital in Chandigarh where they operated upon it, put it in a plaster, and did whatever needed to be done.

When I was released from the hospital I went back home. And there I sat just like before, but now I was totally injured. And not just on my foot. Though less apparent, I had also been hit hard on my head. I didn't feel like going back to that MLA and begging for my job.

The accident changed everything. I remember feeling sorrow that I might never be able to play cricket again with my sons. They were seven and eight at the time. And not only was I physically spent and immobile, but I was badly shaken in my mind.

CHAPTER 18

THE FROZEN SIGNATURE

For a few months I just stayed home. And for once, I had peace. Nobody was asking me to do anything, nobody trying to convince me to rejoin the job. Nobody was creating problems for me.

Then, one day—after I don't know how many months—I was lying on my bed. My wife had just changed the dressing on my foot. It was midafternoon and some people from my department arrived. It was the friend of the MLA who was almost beaten to a pulp on our way to Shimla, he and two others who had worked under me.

At first it seemed they just wanted to sit with me and inquire after my health. But it didn't take long for it to become clear that they had an agenda: yet again, they had come to try to convince me to get myself reinstated so they could put in transfers to work under me. They began with telling me how the new District Commissioner was hell to work under. He treated them like his lackeys and never shared the 'commissions.' Everybody hated him.

They reminded me of how great a team we had been, how we'd gotten our work done and still had one hell of a time. And it was true, we *had* been a great team. In their own way they loved me, and I loved them. We started to reminisce. Then they told me they had already worked it out with the MLA. The papers were ready. I didn't even have to see the MLA. All I had to do was sign the papers, and I'd receive a new posting. Then they would put in transfers so they could work under me. We'd have our old team back, and we could all enjoy again. They started warmly reminiscing about our times together.

In the middle of all this—while lying on my bed with my old colleagues sitting around me recalling the old days—something very strange and disquieting happened. I don't really know what caused it, but I was lying there when suddenly the room flipped upside down and then righted itself. The whole room, it flipped right over, the floor where the ceiling should be and the ceiling under my feet. Although it righted itself the very next moment and obviously must have happened in my mind, as you can imagine it shook me: how could this have happened? And if this could happen, anything could happen. What if I could no longer hold onto space?

They must have seen the sweat appear on my face, and the look in my eye. But how could I tell my colleagues that in the middle of our nostalgic musings the room had suddenly flipped upside down? Instead, I told them I was not well. They could tell I wasn't lying; they got the message and left.

After some months, once I had begun to walk, my junior returned. Maybe someone had told him I had recovered. I suspect there was a conspiracy with my family. He brought the completed papers from the MLA, authorizing me in a new posting. He tried to convince me, telling me how lucky I was that no action had been taken; rather than being punished I was being offered the position of officer in charge of a good sub-division. Everybody started pushing me, my wife, her parents, my parents—they were all working on me.

Before I knew it, it was my first day and my junior was driving me to my new place of posting. Just before we left, my wife handed my junior a bag of fruits. She told him, "If my husband starts to fade, just give him some fruit. It will replenish him." I had no physical reserves whatsoever. I was almost entirely spent. My light could easily have gone out.

After some time, I began to attend the job on my own. I was just going along with what was expected of me. My junior engineers from before got their transfers to work under me. They thought I was OK now that I had rejoined. They thought once I started my job I'd begin enjoying life like before.

The truth was that I was just sitting behind my desk, playacting the role of an SDO, a Sub-Divisional Officer. They'd gather around, discussing the important work at hand, while I looked on as if from a distance, as if I recognized no one. I had always been such a very efficient officer. I could do any work. People would talk about my work with wonder, just like that culvert I told you about, which I completed in a night.

From the outside I may have looked like the same man, a bit worn for illness. But nobody had an inkling of what was going on within me, that I was wrestling with the idea that I just couldn't go on. Everybody was pressuring me to continue. From my family I heard it, from my friends, my colleagues—everybody was making such a gallant effort to convince me to do the right thing and stick to my job. Yet for me the problem was simply how to escape the situation, how to get out of this bind—how to make all these people go away and leave me alone.

My underlings began covering for me. They were doing half the work I was supposed to do, but in reality I was getting nothing done and the work of my division was seriously lagging. Inevitably, this became a problem for my superior who would have to explain to his higher-ups why the work I was assigned wasn't being completed.

But he was afraid to confront me, much less report me, and I knew it. So I told him he was free to write to his bosses and tell them the truth, that *I* was the problem, that I wasn't doing anything and showed no interest in my job. I didn't mind. My superior was a decent man. Why should he get in trouble? But he was afraid of me. Most of the officers in my department were.

It all stemmed from an incident that happened back when I was new in the department, when I was in my mid-twenties. One of the other officers was retiring, and there was a party for him.

In those days I had a huge shiny motorcycle with a throaty roar. It was a Royal Enfield. The model's name was Bullet. But that wasn't the only bullet I owned. As I told you, I also bought a weapon, a revolver, and kept it tucked into my belt, as was a fashion amongst us young men of the Punjab at the time. But it was more than that. It was in our blood.

We Jats of the Punjab have been great warriors since time immemorial. Even now, we have our own regiment in the Indian army and are famous for bravery and gallantry on the field. The Jat Regiment was famous even in the British Army; we fought alongside the Brits in both World Wars. Even before the Brits arrived, we rose up against the Moguls.

When you picture a Jat soldier you see him proud and powerful with an impressive turban riding atop a tall horse, always with a weapon, what we call a *khunda*, a large and exceptionally sharp knife, either in his raised hand or in a sheath by his side. In my generation of young men, the tall horse was replaced by a large motorcycle—and in my case the knife was replaced by a revolver.

I didn't expect to have a quarrel with anyone, but packing a revolver was a matter of pride. It gave one a sense of power; it gave confidence to one's personality. The Punjab in those days was sort of like the Wild West.

I must also confess that back then I had a very strong ego. I was sure of myself in a way that most people of that age aren't. I thought I knew who I was. I've always had this special confidence, perhaps because of this birthmark on my skin and my mother's unaltering conviction that I had direct connection to the Absolute, and that as such my utterances were no less than that of an oracle. I've always had this inborn conviction. But as a young man this definitely led to an oversized image of myself. In other words, I had the feeling I was a somebody and that that somebody was somebody special. I was also a bit crazy.

All the other senior officers were there, people from the head office in Chandigarh, everyone's boss's boss. There were even some politicians. So there was a certain tension in the air. There was also free liquor and I suppose to relieve the tension everyone was getting quite drunk, as men will when there is an open bar.

One of my colleagues sitting near me started giving me trouble. Actually he and the others were all jealous of me because in such a short time I was showing my worth to our superiors. He wanted to pull me down in front of the others, to ridicule and make fun of me, and he chose the easiest route: to make fun of my hearing. He thought this would add to his standing with the head office. There was an opening for some higher position and maybe he thought I was competing with him for it. At any rate, he wanted to downgrade me and get the others laughing. This was clear in the way he talked and gestured in an exaggerated way so I could understand, mocking me the whole while, saying this and that and I can't remember what, but lastly he said, "Why do you always carry that revolver?"

So I took it out. I aimed it at the sky, not really at the sky but just above this man's head, and I fired. I fired all six shots. I wanted to give him something of a scare, to put him in his place, you can say. I shot two or three this way, two that. Just to have fun, but at the same time to teach him something. Understand? Maybe I did it somewhat in anger. But I didn't lose my head. It was deliberate, you can say. Though he didn't know it, he was never in danger. I fired all the shots then tucked it back in my belt with the barrel still hot.

After that, everybody, from the officers on down, was afraid of me. Their attitude was, "Don't touch him. Let him be." As if I were a mad dog—or maybe even a tiger!

That is why my superior was afraid to either push me to get my work done or report me for not doing so. Yet he was a good man and I didn't want to put difficulty into his life. Normally it would have been both his duty, and to his advantage, to confront me for not doing my work—but he didn't. He didn't say a word of complaint. It was conspicuously lacking. And that could only be because he was still afraid of me. He could not understand that I was not the same Vikram that he had known before.

So I told him I wouldn't mind if he reported me to his superiors. I even told him that it was his rightful duty to lay the blame at my feet. "You are free," I told him. "Do as you wish and as you must. I won't even bother denying it."

He could not understand how a man in my position would knowingly fail to perform his most basic duties, and then ask to be reported. I had no way of explaining that some force was pushing me from behind, a force far greater than my own. How could I tell him that we are *all* being pushed from behind, so to speak, part of a greater flow, that we are imbedded in something infinitely greater, a single flow that is carrying us all along. I was being led over the waterfall and though I might have wanted to resist crashing my life, turning so far within that I was turning myself inside out, I was powerless. It was like finding myself in a flooding river. It would have been useless to resist. There is a point at which you stop struggling and you just surrender.

A psychologist might say my unconscious mind had control over me, and it's true that I was being overwhelmed by a force whose origins were beyond my conscious mind. But to me the unconscious includes *everything* that is not conscious, and we are conscious of so little. Doesn't the unconscious include the entire sea in which our island of consciousness floats? Doesn't it reach back to the entire universe, to all that is beyond our grasp and our powers of understanding? As I see it, the unconscious includes everything that we do not know and cannot grasp, all that is not available to our conscious minds, all those influences that are greater than us, including the great sweep of time beginning with the singularity of the Big Bang and all it set in motion and is now playing itself out. So you can say it was the universe itself that was pushing me from behind towards some unknown goal, to reach which I apparently had to purge myself of myself. I had no choice. I had to accept it. It was inevitable that things would come to a pass, that I would again reach a crossroads.

I always knew, right from when I first joined all those years earlier, that one day I would leave the job. My junior engineer at that time was a wise man. Though junior to me, he was elder and had been there a long time and knew the ropes. He was sort of my advisor also, initiating me into the subtle and arcane world of bribery and corruption.

There were contracts for building projects large and small—we call them tenders—that were put out for bids. My superiors in Chandigarh would not interfere—not as long as a fair cut was offered them. This was a game that had rules. By knowing the rules of the game, my junior engineer told me, I could prosper.

He let me know just how lucrative my newly gained position could be if I were smart about it, what level of wealth and position I could gain. On the one hand I was fascinated, tempted by the future he was dangling before me; on the other, I was afraid of what it would do to me. Not only would I be entering that world of corruption; at the same time I knew that world of corruption would be entering into me.

I remember how he laughed when I used to tell him with conviction during my first months on the job that I would not retire one day but quit.

"This is what everyone says when they first take the job and realize the webs one is forced to enter," he said, "the compromises the job demands. They always think they will leave it. But no one ever does. I've never seen it—not once the money begins flowing, not once they get used to the status and position, the wealth and assets they can easily build up. Most get addicted to the power they wield over others."

At that time I said to him, with a conviction that must have seemed mysterious, "Mark my words: I will not leave the job, but the job will yet be left by me. It will not be in my hands." Don't ask how I knew this from the beginning, but it is exactly how it came to pass.

I was still coming to the office, but I was increasingly unable to give any attention to my work. There was a tension building up inside me. It all came to a head one fine day when I was sitting behind my desk looking out the window and my clerk entered my office with some papers for me to sign. This was routine and almost a ritual. It happened several times a day that my clerk would enter and place a stack of papers before me on the desk. It used to be that I would scrutinize each document before signing, but for a while now I hadn't bothered. He would place the papers before me on my desk and I would sign them as quickly as possible—just to get them, and him, out of the way.

As usual, he placed the papers before me and stood looking over my shoulder. I lifted my pen—but my hand refused to obey; it refused to sign. You can say my subconscious mind had taken over. But if the subconscious reaches back to the entire universe, to what they call God, then maybe it was God himself that stopped me. It was some deeper and stronger force that I had no control over. For whatever reason, my hand got paralyzed, not really paralyzed, but my hand refused to obey my order to sign.

After a few awkward moments, the pen frozen in my hand, my clerk standing over my desk becoming confused, I thundered, "Take these damn documents away and bring me a blank piece of paper. Get me a clean sheet!"

He did so, and I picked up a pen, the same pen, and wrote the date across the top of the page. Then I wrote the following line: "I, Vikram Singh, Sub-Divisional Officer for the Punjab Public Works Department, hereby resign from the job, effective at this moment." I signed it, and gave it to my clerk.

What I really felt like writing was, "Go to hell, all of you—and leave me alone!"

"Send it to anybody you want," I told him. "Do with it as you will. I am done with this job."

I had my driver bring the car, and had him drive me the fifty some-odd miles to my home. Then I sent the car away. And that was the last I saw of my job or my department. It was finished, for all time to come.

Usually, when people leave the job, they feel like staying at least loosely attached to their department. But for me it stopped existing. I didn't bother to hear who was rising through the ranks, what big projects were in the works, who was doing what. That was the end of it.

Now home, I had again to face that perennial question: What am I going to do with my bloody life!

CHAPTER 19

TIME'S DISINTEGRATION

For a short time, maybe for just an afternoon, I actually considered becoming a baba. Just to stick it to all those who had imposed the persona of a saint upon me. In India being a baba, a holy man, a saint is a respected position in life—you could even call it a profession. With the experiences I'd had, and the reading I had done, I easily could have been a success. Words of wisdom are not that hard to spout. I spouted them all the time. In fact, my wife used to complain of precisely that.

Every time I started talking of spiritual things, things about religion, when I clothed in that garb the thoughts I was having, and yes even speaking as if I were some sort of baba myself, my wife would cut me short with some rational argument. She would tell me that I was nobody to speak like a baba. Every single time, she'd crop me down to size. It was good for me. She didn't allow me to be a baba even in my subconscious mind. She would scream: "Listen to me and remember: you are not a baba! Don't talk like that. Not in front of me!" My wife was my greatest critic. My eldest son was second; my younger son, though less vociferous, was third—and on down the line. But my wife was always the first in the line. She was my equal and my critic. That helped me.

But it wasn't really my wife's prodding that stopped me from becoming a baba. It was my own temptations. I told myself that so long as I figured my eye would linger on some beautiful girl that came for guidance, as long as the thought would arise, "Ah, what a beautiful girl," so long as I thought that in such a situation my eye would still linger, I vowed not to become a baba. And I've kept that pledge to this day!

What I did do, after some time, was start a business with my nephew, my eldest sister's son. There was a new type of brick kiln, known as a mechanized brick kiln, which was just being developed and had the potential to produce bricks at a fraction of the cost. This new method was partly untried and had technicalities still to be worked out. Since I was an engineer, I could do this work. So you could say mine was the brain behind this kiln. I advised my nephew what to do and he did it; in a short time it became hugely successful. This was good for me since I was able to feed myself and my family. It also gave me a way of fending off those who were always pestering me about what I was going to do in lieu of a job now that I had permanently thrown away the best job anyone could imagine. I had an answer now to shut them up: "I've become a businessman."

Looking back, I can see that I threw myself into the project for distraction, to get rid of myself and all those questions. I was entirely in the dark and didn't ask for what was happening to me. Yet I couldn't change my course. Most of the time I was not well— neither physically nor mentally. Sometimes I was seeing strange flashes of light that made me question my perception.

As always, I had tremendous energy, but I was so lost inside myself that I could only partly engage with the work. As soon as the kiln was up and running smoothly, I lost all interest in it. Creating it was one thing; maintaining and running it as a profitable business was another. I sold my nephew my share, and as the business prospered he paid me back in installments. With this I was able to maintain my family. And to this day that kiln which I started is making my nephew a wealthy man.

All I've ever wanted is a little cash in my pocket to see to my daily needs. I've never been interested in assets. My nephew is rich in his way, with property; I'm rich in mine. My total assets are in my bag. Nobody can understand my riches. It is as if I have the whole universe.

My nephew was uneducated. And even though my ideas and the effort I put into the kiln made him a rich man, you know what I say? When you do some kindness, throw it in the river. Forget it. I have never felt responsible for doing kindness to anybody. Even in the department, I never felt as if I helped somebody—a contractor, a colleague, or an underling—even though when deals came through I often rewarded those around me with a greater cut than was their due. He got what he deserved, either from me or you could say by nature, through me, by means of the one flow. So I never felt I have done anything for anybody. That way, if later the person doesn't reciprocate or pay me back it never bothers me—it doesn't even cross my mind. He gets his due, I get mine. Everybody is getting whatever he or she deserves, including me.

Even if I help somebody who otherwise would have died of hunger, this is just how things are going. No thanks is owed me. That is what my experience revealed: there is only one story, one flow. Somebody is giving, somebody else is receiving: it isn't two separate stories. The entire universe—it is all one story.

When I quit that kiln, it was not in my hands to continue. Not only was I at least partly out of my senses: my health was failing me too. So I could not continue. I had to sell my share, though I couldn't explain. How to express what was going on inside me and why I was acting as I was?

My nephew, wife, family, friends—none of them had a clue what was really happening, that I was undergoing some other process, trying to get back to that state beyond all this coming and going. And since nothing short of this would give me peace, I was compelled, forced you could almost say, to dig deeper and not stop until I uncovered the living foundation I had tasted in that experience, which had lingered, setting fire to my search.

Again, we stumble on words. It isn't really true what I just said, that I was *trying* to reach anywhere. In fact, at the time, if anything, I felt forced from behind. No matter how much I might have wanted to live a normal life, I was prevented. I was being stripped clean, pushed to my limit. I might have wished it otherwise. It was like reaching some sort of warp speed, or approaching the sound barrier; things start to vibrate; then they begin to shake most violently, and you fear you might fall to pieces.

Yet what being was ever born from an egg without cracking its shell?

The egg has a germ of life within it, a potential. With time, a chick develops within the shell. The shell provides both protection and the horizon of the known world. It is the young bird's nature to outgrow its shell and struggle against it. The shell, which to this point provided needed protection, whose inner surface marked the limit of the known, the encompassing horizon, will one day become an impediment that needs to be broken and left behind. It is not that dissimilar to when a caterpillar becomes a butterfly by breaking out of its chrysalis and enters an entirely new element.

The chick still enclosed in its shell, perhaps growing too big for it, will not at first understand the nature of what confines it. How could it know "shell" when it has no way of knowing that the space in which its germ has come to life is not the entire universe, but the interior of a confined space? How could it know that a hugely expansive world lies just outside the thinnest of veils? The shell, which is all we see from the outside when holding an egg, doesn't even exist for the young developing bird! As the bird develops, it will naturally feel the impulse to break out of what was once protecting, but is now confining it.

Children becoming adolescents are in a similar situation. And just as children in their rebellion might make mistakes, so the young bird, might not know at first what tool it has at its disposal to break the shell. Not understanding the nature of its shell, it may first try by pressing its downy wings against the inner surface of the shell to crack it open. How is the unhatched bird to know what those wings are really for—to fly through an openness of space neither knowable nor imaginable before it cracks out of the shell and makes that quantum leap into the airy world? It cannot at first know that the wings' soft feathers are useless for breaking the shell.

Birds are born with what's called an egg tooth, a sharp little protuberance attached to the tip of the bill. It is a tool especially for chipping the escape hatch. Isn't it fantastic that a sharp protruding pick is provided especially for this task of transformation, and that it falls off a few days after hatching? All birds have this, and even reptiles, who also hatch from eggs. It is provided by nature. Just knowing that solutions are also provided gave me courage. No matter how terrifying my experiences, on some level I knew that I need not worry.

I had the confidence that I could do no wrong, which doesn't mean I wasn't stumbling in the dark, making poor decisions. Yet I was not wrong in doing what I did. You cannot say something is right or wrong. There are no other possible scenarios. Things are exactly what they are. That is what the insight teaches. That's how it is from the perspective of the One. Here in the East we call it "the perfect unfolding."

The bird fluttering its wings to break its shell is also not wrong. It is doing what is in its nature to do at the time. Learning by failing. Growing. That is how it works, the evolution of living beings. It cannot be otherwise.

What is right at one stage can also be wrong at another. But each serves its purpose. Like the boy who used to enjoy his parents' protection suddenly finding their embrace suffocating as he reaches the cusp of young manhood and feels within himself the need to break away. Is it that different from the chick struggling against the hard shell, seemingly impossible to break shortly before the time comes for it to use its egg tooth—almost miraculously there exactly when he needs it—to break free and assume its winged existence?

I, adult though I was, was in much the same position as that chick, and, like the chick, I didn't know it. The beak in my case, the weapon of choice, was the sharp question with which I was trying to break the shell that now confined me: Who am I, and why have I come to this earth? I had enjoyed life to the hilt in the last eight years, not giving a damn what I fed my body with, how much I drank and whether I smoked two or three packs of cigarettes a day.

The last cigarette I ever smoked almost killed me. I guess it had to happen. Something had to give. I was smoking a cigarette when my heart went blub-blub-blub. It was like a pump that had gotten blocked. I was rushed to the hospital in Chandigarh and they said it was a miracle that I was still alive. "Your cholesterol level is off the charts," they told me. The doctor gave me some medicine to reduce cholesterol and to thin the blood, for this and that. I was told to report for surgery to unlock the clogged artery.

I went home, and after three or four days I threw the medicines away. I knew these medicines could not cure my true malady. If there was no ultimate unchanging underlying layer to this play on the senses, then what was the purpose of being here? It would all end and vanish, nothing into nothingness. I suppose I was desperate. I thundered it out to the heavens: What for? Why have I come to this earth?!

What was happening in my body was just a reflection of my crisis within. And I was as inept as that chick within its shell fluttering its wings and expecting a crack to form.

What cracks must be a shell, and from the outside I must have seemed but a shell of a man. Human beings can go through great changes, quantum jumps, transformations, stages. I began to see it like this; it became a useful framework.

I had been reading in modern physics how they'd reduced everything in the universe to the play of four fundamental forces: gravity, the electro-magnetic force, the strong nuclear force, and the weak nuclear force. Though beyond my field of expertise, which was engineering, I started reading deeply into physics.

Until the mid-1800s there had been five forces. The electrical and magnetic forces were thought to be separate. Then it was James Maxwell, a Scotsman, who discovered that electrical currents had an effect on magnetic fields, that you could actually turn magnetic force into electric force and vice versa. Through experimentation and a keen eye, he saw, and later proved, that electric and magnetic forces are one—the electromagnetic.

For well over a century now the goal of physicists, their holy grail, has been to find a Unified Field Theory which would reduce the remaining four forces to one. They are searching for a single set of equations that would explain everything and describe the workings of the entire universe. Einstein dedicated much of his life to the search, and failed—as has everyone since.

It was clear, from my perspective, from the perspective of the One, that they would never get there, that the rational mind can only get you so far. It is as if rationality works perfectly well on solid ground, like an automobile that can take you anywhere, from here in the Himalayas all the way down to India's southern tip. But when you reach the sea and you want to get to Sri Lanka, another vehicle is needed, a boat, built according to other principles, made to float on water and withstand not hills and bumps on a road, but waves, currents, and winds on the surface of a dynamically moving fluid.

In no way do I doubt the power and truth of rationality, and its expression, Newtonian physics. You better know and accord with these laws of falling bodies, force and counterforce when building bridges and dams. I certainly did as an engineer. These laws undoubtedly work. How else could skyscrapers be built? Engineering figures are now fed into computers, which crunch numbers and spit out design parameters. But ever since that patent clerk, Albert Einstein, came up with his Theory of Relativity, we know the world as described by Newton, his Clockwork Universe of strict cause and effect, of straight lines stretching out to infinity, is but an approximation, relatively true within certain parameters. It is as if, to use our recently used analogy, Newtonian physics works on land but not on water. It applies at a certain scale, that of our everyday experience, of millimeters and miles. It describes the behavior of an appearance.

Einstein's equations also apply to our everyday world; but on the scale of the everyday the effect is so minute that we can safely disregard them and get on with the building of dams and bridges as if Newton's word was final. It is when considering interstellar space that one must consider the fluidity of time and space and things get topsy-turvy. Time slows and stops as speeds increase and approach the speed of light. Space turns into time. Matter and energy are understood to be one; they are both manifestations of the same matrix which, since 1908, physicists have called spacetime. Time and space are interchangeable aspects of a single whole. The faster you move through space, especially as you approach the speed of light, the slower time flows until it ceases entirely. It is what happens if you catch a ride on a beam of light.

Every historical age is limited by a horizon. Even our age of reason, of rational thought and action, of scientific thinking, while astoundingly effective, had its genesis and will one day be superseded. Just as it took a new mode of thinking, based on the strict adherence to evidence and clear rational thought, to displace the cosmology of the medieval Catholic church and to rightly place the sun at the center of our solar system, so, I believe, the scientific method will also be superseded.

I am well aware that saying this is a heresy in this day and age. At least they don't still burn heretics at the stake. That's what Galileo was up against when he proclaimed the earth moves around the sun and not the other way around. His only way to escape the inquisition was to submit to the orthodoxy of the day and to write a decree forever renouncing the heliocentric theory. He did this, knowing full well that neither the Church nor his renunciation would have any effect on the earth and its yearly circle around the sun!

Most people, most rational people, the people of our age, would balk if with an all-knowing wink I told them there is something beyond the strictly rational, evidence-based framework of our day. They'd think I'd want to revert to the Dark Ages from which we came before the European enlightenment, which has swept the world. They'd immediately accuse me of advocating a devolution to superstition and religious mumbo-jumbo, a return to the swamp of fuzzy thinking that our rational, scientific age has just so laboriously extricated us from. Yet it is impossible to explain intellectually, through numbers, that we come from the One and it is to the One that we shall return, that this world of seeming dualities, of separate beings and objects—nucleons, electrons, and the rest of it—that there is a foundation upon which all this appearance rests.

Rational thought can get you there no more than an automobile that conveys you so effortlessly across an entire continent can ferry you across the water. For that you need a vehicle suited to the new medium. You must make a jump. That is why I was so enthused by modern physics, which speaks of quantum jumps. Sometimes an increase in knowing is not a matter of degree, but of kind.

Our way of thought sticks to us. It isn't easy to see that our way of thinking, the so-called foundation upon which we gaze at the world and come to understanding, is conditional and not necessarily foundational. The fact that societies tend to be comprised of people all thinking in a similar way is quite natural and not surprising. We are all conditioned by the times in which we live and the educations we receive—to such a degree that we doubt there are other ways of seeing.

We are like fish in the sea wondering what it means to be wet. Science is now our measure. It is our main organ of knowing, the way we come to know the world and our place in it. Yet this has not always been, and I don't believe it will forever be.

What is science? It is sometimes useful to get to the root meaning of a word or concept by following the word's etymology. And when we examine the word 'science' we see it goes back through some old forms of French to Latin words for knowledge and knowing. But if we follow it back further, if we go back to the Greek and Indo-European roots, we find the word science has for its origin words for 'cut,' 'divide,' and 'separate.' It goes back to the same Greek root, *skhizein*, meaning to cut or split that brings us to schizophrenic, the mind divided against itself.

Our age is one of rationality, founded on dividing wholes and comparing the parts, reducing the universe and all the stars in it to numbers, and then calculating the differences between them in order to predict their behavior and divine their origins. Yet if you add up any amount of numbers—even if you add up every single number out there—you'll never reach infinity!

To go against the prevailing way of thought can be lonely—and quite dangerous. Everyone thought I had gone seriously off the rails. And in a way I had. I was reaching bottom, my core, uncertain whether I was entering almost a state of madness.

CHAPTER 20

RAMANA MAHARSHI &
VINCENT VAN GOGH

Occasionally, and mostly just to pass the time, to get my mind focused, I would pick up a book. They would sort of come to me. One day I found a book called *Samadhi*. *Samadhi* is what we in the East call complete liberation, enlightenment. It was written by Mouni Sadhu. Mouni means silent, and a sadhu is a wandering holy man. So the man who wrote the book was known as the Silent Sadhu. What a funny world, I thought. How is it possible for a silent man to fill so many pages with words? And especially on the topic of *samadhi*, which no words can express? I was curious, but mostly I was just looking for a way to pass the time.

It turned out that book had a strong effect on my life—even though I never got past the first page. It also had quite an effect on my eldest son. The book starts by paying homage to the man he called "the modern Great Rishi of India," Ramana Maharshi.

How to describe what ran through me when I read that name, Ramana Maharshi? There was something in the way the name rolled off the tongue. The author called him a modern rishi. The word rishi is reserved not just for any realized being, not just any sadhu. The term rishi is reserved only for the most highly realized human beings, like the ones who wrote the Vedas.

Who was this man, this Ramana Maharshi?

Soon, and quite by chance, another book came into my hands, this one a collection of Ramana's sayings. A short introduction sketched his life, how he was born in the late 1870s in South India. One afternoon, in his sixteenth year, he had a sudden premonition of death. He became numb and felt death creep over his body. He lay down on his bed and surrendered. In one go he experienced the complete annihilation of his ego, you could say, which we in the East call total illumination.

Having had this experience, there was no question of him continuing the normal life of a schoolboy. So he ran away to the precincts of the sacred mountain in the southern state of Tamil Nadu, Arunachala, where he lived in a series of caves. Over time, an ashram formed around him, to which people came from all over the world. He became known as the greatest living sage of India. He died there in 1950.

Once I heard of this sacred mountain in the south, I knew I had to go. I wanted to experience the atmosphere where this great rishi had lived and died. I stayed in the Ramana Ashram, but mostly I walked the trail that circles the mountain, which rises so abruptly from the plains.

It took many hours to circumambulate that mountain, and as I walked, I ruminated over Ramana's teaching. I was trying to get to the heart of one particular statement that Ramana made, recorded in one of the books: "The question 'Who am I?' is not really meant to get an answer, the question 'Who am I?' is meant to dissolve the questioner."

I was quite desperate in those days. The intensity of my quest increased as my search became more hopeless. I was failing in my body and in my mind. Yet I felt being in the presence of that mountain was good for me. Therefore, when I learned that some industrialist was starting a boarding school nearby, which was supposed to rival the best boarding schools in Dehradun and Darjeeling, I got my eldest son enrolled. This gave me ample excuse to go down there, either when dropping him off or when picking him up. He was a little young for boarding school and was often homesick. So I'd go there just to visit him. And when I did, I'd often then spend a month at nearby Arunachala, mostly circling the holy mountain and calling out for help.

It got so bad that back in the Punjab I'd be looking out my window at the rooftops of adjacent buildings or at the brick wall opposite, and these things would no longer be made of brick or the materials that roofs are made of. Rather, they were comprised of dashes—dashes and flashes of light, multi-colored light, like strokes of a painter's brush. A red brick wall was not only made of flashes and dashes and strokes of red light, but there were purple flashes, green, dashes of every color of the rainbow, which together created the impression of a solid red wall. I might have been going mad.

It was only later that I saw Vincent van Gogh paintings and was astounded to see on his canvases what I had seen with my own eyes—the flashes and strokes of colored light. Then I read how van Gogh had lost his mind—maybe by sunstroke, or was it syphilis? At any rate, his life was difficult and he lost his mind. I was somewhat near that position. Perhaps I was saved by that experience of eight years earlier, when I got one foot anchored on the other shore. Without that, maybe I also would not have made it back. The road within is littered with such cases. What happened to van Gogh could easily have happened to me.

Sometimes I'd be sitting there with my wife or my nephew and it would happen. The solid world around me would be transformed into strokes of multi-colored light and flashes of energy. It was as if the whole thing was pulsing. How could I tell them I was experiencing the world not as solid objects, but as concretions of vibrating energy? They'd think me stark raving mad! You might also have thought me mad had you met me then.

By leaving the job and doing nothing in lieu of it, I interrupted, midstream, the course a man is meant to take in this world, especially if he has a wife and children—like having a profession and taking on a certain role in society commensurate with it. I had already cast off one set of expectations, imposed upon me by my birthmark, that I was a holy-man and was in thick with the gods. By having already once pried myself loose from an adjective, perhaps it was easier for me than for the common man to do so again. The trick is to put that wedge between you and your role, between who you've been led to believe you are and who you might really be. It opens the possibility for a transformation to take place.

This is not without cost or danger. We are talking about leaving the clearing our society carves out of the void, with all its norms of behavior and notions of right and wrong, and setting out alone into the trackless jungle. We are talking about breaking the spell of our times, freeing ourselves from the mind of our contemporaries.

Tremendous energy is bound up in established forms. Our familial roles, our professions, our economic standing, what religion or ethnic group we happen to belong to, our nation, whether we are high or low—whatever it is, our role in the world locks in a tremendous portion of our psychic energy. Born as free and spontaneous beings, we become locked in. With time, we take on a more or less conventional role. Energy gets locked in form. We can hardly imagine the grip with which this role holds and molds us until we perceive a crack. Einstein's famous equation tells us a tremendous amount of energy is locked inside the atom; when released it obliterates entire cities from this earth.

One risks the danger of being set adrift between states, getting stuck in what the Tibetans call the *bardo*, that place in-between. And that is where I was. Staring into space. Cut off. I must have looked half mad.

But rather than going mad, I was breaking out of the madness that civilization imposes upon us all. It was like trying to break the sound barrier. No matter how it appeared from the outside or how it might sound to you now, and despite my loved ones' quite justified fear for my life, I was not mad.

Space, I already told you, looked like dashes. But there were other things too. Sometimes I'd be sitting there and time itself would slow—the very flow of time, the pacing of it, the space between the tickings of the clock. Time was slowing and threatening to stop. I feared falling between the cracks and finding myself outside of the flow of time entirely.

Everyone knows what is meant by a minute, a second, or an hour. Everyone can snap their fingers to the approximate beat of one second. We all know the difference between that and what is meant by an hour.

What happened to me was this: I'd be sitting with someone or sometimes by myself when suddenly I'd feel as if I was becoming stuck in time. Time didn't really stop, but the flow of time slowed.

The ticking of a clock measures an even flow of time. Yet our perception of time can vary. Sitting with your lover, an hour can pass in seconds. Hit your thumb with a hammer and a minute can seem an hour. But it wasn't like that. It was not my *percep-tion* of time, but time itself that was altering. That's what was so frightening. I feared finding myself imprisoned like a fly in amber, stuck because time had ceased to flow.

There may be no fear greater than that of being stuck in time.

It felt like being in a raft tumbling over a waterfall, like a body falling into nothingness, tumbling through endless space. Could this be what it's like to be dead? Will I not be free, even after my death? I'd always thought death brings, if nothing else, at least release. Don't we say the dead are 'resting in peace'? Could it be possible to fall out of time and not be free? Is this what was happening?

Having expended everything, there was nothing left. I was passing through the Valley of Death, locked into a frame of space and time that brought me unspeakable terror. As humans, we are imprisoned—imprisoned in a very narrow place. The claustrophobia of the human condition overwhelmed me, and I was seized with panic. Having tried to free myself, still I found myself bound. Will I not be free, even after my death? Time was slowing and threatening to stop. Something was still binding me. No words can describe the panic I felt, the terror of it.

We use words to break the isolation. When I reached my crisis I felt lost inside myself—just as one may feel lost in a jungle, in a forest. I was imprisoned in my ego. I had no one to speak with. I was cut off from nature, from all others. And I was imprisoned in myself. I felt lost, as if I was going mad. If only I could have told others of my situation: I am here! I am somebody, and I am here. Just as a person lost in a jungle would try to convey the situation, to say, in whatever way, I am here.

It is in this way that man, when he was still in the jungle and felt locked into his own self, into his own ego, and he felt lonely, it is in this way that the jungle man started language. Maybe this is how it all began: we created the world at the same time we created the I—and then we felt alone.

We called out, just to hear if there was anybody else out there and if we might not get a response in order to make sense of our surroundings, to break the isolation. We created communication to find our relation with the other human being, with nature,

with animals—with everything. This is a lion! This is a mountain! This is a stream! We gave a word to everything so we could
make sense of it, to communicate with each other and achieve
some peace.

We are still in the same situation as the man or woman in
the jungle. It is going on to this day, even though we live in cities. The difference is that now we have developed all means of
communication—telephone, books, radio, Internet, Facebook,
right up to satellites and fiber optics sending messages around
the world at the speed of light. We use these means to convey
our situation and to feel less alone. It is ultimately to relieve that
feeling of being lost that all these means of communication have
been developed.

My body could easily have given out right then and there.
Death could have claimed me without further notice. But I knew
if I died—if my existence in time and space ceased—that something would still be clinging to me. I would still be attached to
some thought. And if something is sticking to you, you are not
free: you cannot pass through the eye of the needle.

In Jesus' parable he says it would be easier for a camel to pass
through the eye of a needle than for a rich man to enter the Kingdom of Heaven. Even though Jesus instructs the rich man to give
away all his riches in order to 'enter heaven,' the actual problem
lies not in the riches themselves.

The bars of gold are practically irrelevant.

What's important is the rich man's *attachment* to his gold,
perhaps even his *identification* with it. This goes for whatever we
identify with, whatever role we play.

CHAPTER 21

THE FAKIR AND THE KING

There is a story out of the East about a fakir and a king. A fakir is an ascetic, a baba, sadhu, what we might also call a saint. Usually fakirs are of the Muslim faith, but perhaps you could even say it was what they were trying to make of me. This fakir lived a very austere life outside the strictures of the common man. In other words, he was spontaneous and never gave a damn for this world's do's or don'ts.

He lived in the Himalayas or someplace far away. His possessions consisted of a walking stick from the jungle, a dried gourd for carrying water, and an old patch of cloth that he used to clothe himself, and to protect from inclement weather. He ate what came his way, and drank from streams and wells. He was known to meditate under old trees far from human settlement. Word began to spread that he was the real thing, a god-realized man—which even in ancient India was rare.

Eventually, word reached the king that such a man was living in his kingdom. He heard that even though the fakir possessed nothing and lived like an animal in the jungle, whoever met him came away thinking he was the happiest and most contented person alive. This made the king, by far the richest man in the kingdom, secretly envy the fakir.

You might think a king would have a surfeit of happiness since he could fulfill his every wish with all that treasure and power. The common man might even envy the king for having in abundance what the rest of us must struggle for. But despite his luxurious life and the absolute power with which he ruled his kingdom, happiness had so far eluded the king. He was always wanting, always yearning for something more, something that would bring true contentment. Could this fakir have the key to what all his luxury, power, and position was yet to deliver?

He sent his ministers to go find the fakir in his mountain retreat and to bring him to the palace. When they returned empty handed, saying the ascetic refused to come, the king did not get angry. He took it all in stride, knowing fakirs' behavior is sometimes inscrutable. It is part of their charm. He decided to go himself to the fakir's mountain hideaway.

The king had a plan. He would go to the fakir's retreat and test the fakir himself by inviting him to come live in his palace. Knowing the strange ways of fakirs, the king expected him to refuse. After all, fakirs are famous for preferring poverty to riches, the simple life close to the elements to the cushioned life of the palace. That was part of the king's interest in the fakir. He thought, especially if he was a real fakir, that he would refuse him with some wise words, perhaps a riddle, which would provide a clue, a key to the fulfillment he sought.

But the fakir surprised the king. When the king invited the fakir to the palace, the fakir didn't miss a beat. "OK," he said. "Let us go!" Taking up his walking stick and drinking gourd, his only possessions apart from that cloth wrapped around his loins, he asked the king to lead the way. This made the king suspicious. The king decided to watch the fakir closely once they arrived at the palace to see whether he was the real thing, a truly wise man.

He gave the fakir a suite of sumptuous rooms and had a beautiful set of clothing brought to him. The king thought if he was a real fakir, he would renounce these luxuries. But the man started manifestly enjoying them, along with the rich food, drink, and all the perks you can imagine would be yours if you were the personal guest of a king. But much to the king's distress, the fakir was obviously enjoying life to the fullest!

A month passed. Two months passed. The king kept thinking the fakir would say it was time for him to go back to the jungle, that this life was not for him. But he just kept enjoying the king's hospitality with tremendous gusto. Now he was drinking, keeping company with women, enjoying feasts. Before long, the fakir became fat and the king grew highly suspicious: "Was he only pretending when I met him in the forest? Have I been deceived into taking a charlatan into my palace?"

The more the fakir enjoyed himself, the more miserable the king became, until finally the king confronted him: "When I met you in the forest I was impressed by your austere lifestyle and the depth of your self-denial. Now I see that you are rather like me, denying yourself no pleasure whatsoever. So tell me, what is the real difference between you and me?"

The fakir smiled. He was silent a moment. And then he said, "I will give you your answer in the morning."

The next morning the fakir appeared before the king dressed only in the rag in which he came, holding his walking stick and gourd.

"I am leaving, to where I know not. And I will not be back. Come with me. Let us leave this palace and all these riches behind. Come. Let us go wandering! We need never return."

"But you know I cannot do that!" the king said, sputtering. He hardly knew what to say. He was king. He had great responsibilities, stores of treasure to protect. One day he'd have to groom a son as his successor. And besides, he had grown up with such riches and didn't want to lose them.

"There is the answer to your question," the fakir said. "Because I am not attached to them, I can enjoy all manner of luxuries and leave them whenever I want. Apparently, you cannot. Here is the answer to your question of what is the difference between us."

The king realized the fakir's wisdom and begged him to stay, but the fakir only laughed. He turned, and without a backwards glance walked out of the palace gates—and was never seen again.

CHAPTER 22

EMPTYING

I started reading far and wide, from physics, mysticism, and ancient Sanskrit texts, right up to the Advaita, or non-dual, teachings of Ramana Maharshi. And I also read about psychoanalysis. Of particular interest was self-psychoanalysis, and I got the idea of self-psychoanalyzing myself by watching my thoughts. If I sat quietly and observed what sort of thoughts spontaneously arose, I thought it would give me an idea of what was hidden in my unconscious mind. And if I knew what was in my unconscious mind, I could perhaps free myself from the thoughts that were clinging to me.

There are many definitions of the unconscious. Freud saw it as the repository of one's personal hopes and fears. Jung spoke of the Collective Unconscious, the repository of humanity's mythic archetypes, arising spontaneously and affecting the way we act. As I said before, what I mean by the unconscious mind goes even further back, to the entire universe—right to the Big Bang and all the forces it set in motion, which are now playing themselves out and to whose tune we dance. Sometimes we do things and we don't quite know why we do them. We even do or say things we might not want to. At these times we say we had no choice. We say some unconscious impulse made us do it, some little devil in our minds. We feel as if we were pushed from behind.

Right from the beginning, I knew that I would leave my job. When it happened it seemed I had no choice, as if I had no free will, as if something greater was playing itself out. Some would say it was just my unconscious mind that made me do this or that—as if the unconscious mind is not a very great thing, stretching back to the whole universe! There is only one flow, and

we are all part of it. While most people understand that unconscious thoughts can cause our actions, can push us to do this or
that, I say the universe pushed me!

What I call self-psychoanalysis is perhaps what is really
meant by meditation in the East. I took my cue from Ramana
Maharshi. He said the way to stop the endless flow of thoughts is
to stop taking interest in them.

What I did was this: I simply watched my thoughts. A thought
would arise and I would watch it. And watching it, it would disappear. As long as you give it no energy, as long as you don't engage
with it, whenever a thought is simply observed it will begin to leave
you. If you counter or argue with the thought—if you engage with
it, if you take up its offer—you will give it power and it will not leave
you. You will give it life and it will come back another time, it will
recur, again and again. That thought—now you can call it a problem—will stick to you. This is how most people spend their lives.

But if you watch as a thought arises, if you merely observe the
thought without engaging with it, it will simply leave. It might
come back once or twice, but then it will not come back. In this
way the thoughts leave you one by one.

Perhaps some months passed in this way. I started out doing this exercise while sitting quietly with eyes closed, as if in
meditation. It was easier this way to watch the thoughts arising without distraction. But soon I was able to do the same while
passing through my day. Whatever thought was watched, it
would go away, it would leave me—right out of my head.

There began to be gaps of no thought, as the spaces between
the thoughts widened. I began to glimpse what is there when
there is no thought, only awareness, the matrix from which
thoughts arise, the background, the cloth from which experience
is sewn. Words cannot be applied to this matrix. One must experience it, and then one will know.

This technique provided me a wedge to separate myself from
myself, you could say. It might sound schizophrenic, but I assure
you it is not. It is the sanest thing we can do, especially for those
of us who have had a glimpse, no matter how fleeting, of this matrix, this mother of all things, the ground from which all of this
and that arises.

It is really quite simple: the ability to directly and persistently experience what I am here calling the matrix is what is meant in the East by enlightenment or liberation, the mystics' goal. Nothing else to it. So simple, yet so easily confounded by our habitual mind, forever splitting the One into two, forever placing a wedge between the one thinking and that which is thought, giving birth to the world as we experience it.

The creation of the world did not occur in some distant past. It is happening right now, this birthing of the many from the One. But it is different from other happenings in that there was never a time before it, and there will never be a time after. There's a paradox for you! *Now* presupposes a *then*, a before and an after. Perhaps a now without a before or an after is what they call eternity. If it never ends, there is no after. And with no after, how can there be a before? It is too simple to be easily realized, too much the ocean in which we swim.

By loosening oneself from identification with one's thoughts, one gains glimpses of the fertile ground from which thoughts arise. It is the being at the heart of becoming. That which is. It is rather like when daytime is extinguished with the setting of the sun and the window opens to the deep starry night.

On the one hand a new insight was dawning within me, and on the other I was ridding myself of my previous thoughts, what was in my subconscious mind. I was going to the bottom. Disintegrating. I was ridding myself of everything.

Someone less stable than I could easily have gone mad, but I was anchored by that previous experience. Somehow, I knew I couldn't fail. I've always had this confidence.

Rather than going mad, I was getting rid of the *worldly* madness, the madness of life in the world. I was doing so—and I can laugh about it now—to come to my *own* form of madness!

A twig puts forth a bud, which can open into either a leaf or a flower. This is growth, an elongation or continuation, the building of one thing upon another. But the origin of a new being is something else entirely. New beings are born not of a continuation, a further growth, but of a singularity, when all the forces merge into a single point and dissolve. Out of the nothing, out of the tiniest spark, the spark of life you could say, comes the birth of a new being. That is what it means to give birth to new life. That is the spark of life within the seed; it is the impetus behind the cells first dividing within an egg.

Within myself I was exhausted, finished. My body was broken and I felt not as if I was dying—but as if I was already dead. And finding myself dead and realizing I was still not free—that's when the terror overtook me, that even in death I would not find release and therefore there was no escape. That was when time began to stop for me, to flow like molasses.

It was like being in a cocoon. How else does this earth give birth to a butterfly than by a worm dying to its old self to become something unimaginably new. Human beings are not that different. There are states beyond your present state. Human beings are still evolving.

It was in order to know the past and present state of how we as human beings have understood our place in the universe that I started reading widely in philosophy, mysticism, religion, and physics. For the first time I was encountering the knowledge that physics has reduced the workings of the entire universe to four fundamental forces. I learned about the Big Bang, the singularity out of which the entire universe arose. This stuck to my mind: it was wonderful, all this universe reduced to four forces, starting at a unitary point! Something began to stir, and I began to gain an insight. It became the kernel from which I would write my book, which would occupy me for the next twelve years.

Physicists now tell us that in reality the particles from which atoms are formed don't really exist, that there are no particles, no 'things.' Rather there are relations. The table here, which I can knock with my knuckle, is made of atoms, which as we know are largely made up of empty space. And if we enter the atom and observe the electrons, protons, and neutrons, we can see that this orbital system is as empty as our solar system. And if we study these subatomic particles, these planets and suns of the atoms, things go topsy-turvy, and we enter the strange world of quantum physics, which tells us that these particles cannot be spoken of as existing in themselves but only in relation to the so-called particles surrounding them. Given this intricate web of interconnection, then don't you think maybe a butterfly could flap its wing and change the course of history, as the ancient Chinese philosopher Chuang Tzu mused?

As I went deeper, as I rid my mind of all those thoughts, as my insight into the four forces took hold, as I delved those depths, I also fell deathly ill. My hair turned white in the course of a few weeks, maybe two months at most. That's how long it took to go from jet black to the white that you see today. Not only was my mind emptying, making way for some new knowledge, but my body was ridding itself of the life force that had held it together to that point.

Death and rebirth can happen in this very life. Just as a baby can become a boy and a boy a man, in the same way an adult can turn into something else. Wasn't it one of the ancient Greek philosophers who said, "As the adult is to the child, so the sage is to the adult"? It is rare, but it does occur. It calls for a radical disintegration and reintegration, what could be called a death and rebirth. Didn't Jesus spend forty days in the desert? Didn't Buddha sit alone, fasting under the Bodhi tree? Weren't they visited by demons offering them all the pleasures and wealth the world could provide?

Because it is so rare, most people would say it is fiction, maybe even science fiction, if they heard me say that there is a further stage possible beyond the normal adult stage of the human being. But consider the caterpillar enclosing itself in its cocoon. As it prepares for its transfiguration, shutting itself off from the light, does that worm really know what it is doing, and why? Can the worm imagine its future life with wings? Isn't there some force of nature blindly compelling it to make the transformation?

In my case the dissolution was nearly total, and it included my body. I was giving birth, not only to a new consciousness, but a new body, as if the vessel that held my old self couldn't have held the new. The old vessel had to be gotten rid of. Doesn't the same seed that gives spark to new life first have to wither fully away? Mustn't it find itself buried in the ground, away from the light, for the spark inherent within it to ignite? The seed must come to its singularity; it must die to from where it came and be buried beneath the soil and begin to dissolve. At least the threat of dissolution must be there. According to the physicists, this is just what happened at the birth of the universe, which, having been put into motion by that singularity they call the Big Bang, has been playing itself out for billions of years, unfolding a vast and intricate order of which you and I are a part. Looked at on edge, so to speak, from the perspective of the Big Bang, from the perspective of the One, there is only one flow.

Imagine a creation myth in which 'in the beginning' there was a vast still expanse of water in limitless space, a primordial sea, surface like a mirror, reflecting the sky so perfectly that the sky and its reflection were indistinguishable and therefore were one.

Then came a ripple on the still surface, a formation of little waves. This unevenness, these waves, meant a few things. It meant that they were moving, which means that time was born. Before this, since nothing moved, time would have been irrelevant. It would not have been needed. The other thing that happened is that once waves started moving on the water's surface, the water, instead of reflecting back only the sky, started reflecting the next wave over: the water started reflecting the water back on itself, thinking it was something separate.

From the outside, it must have looked as if I was dying. From within, I felt like a deep-sea diver, exhausting what oxygen I had as I dived deeper and deeper in search of the bottom of the vast ocean where I would find what I was looking for, the golden ring, the reason for my being.

I had abandoned the care of my body to my wife, who was looking after me. Lost in myself, in the depths of a sea where no one could follow, not even attempting to speak of it, I got to the point where I was not even aware of what others were doing around me.

When they saw that I was dying, they called in a succession of doctors. Every time a doctor came, I submitted to his examination—even though I knew it was pointless. How could a doctor cure something he couldn't understand? How could I explain that I was a deep-sea diver, sinking ever further into a fathomless sea, the last slivers of sunlight fading through the gloom above?

But still the doctors came to my home. They examined me and consulted with each other. Specialists were called. They looked at my symptoms, my ashen, sunken face, my disinterest in food, my being oblivious to my surroundings. They heard how within days my hair had all gone gray.

One after another they told my wife they could find no physical source for my condition, no disease or injury to explain my sudden decline. The doctors always gave me medicine, but I never took it. I knew their prescriptions were useless. More than one suggested my problem was psychosomatic and that perhaps a psychiatrist could help. Thank God psychiatrists were rare in those days, at least in our Punjab—or I might have been taken away!

I found out later, much later, through my various researches, that what was happening to me had happened to others. Saint John of the Cross called it the Dark Night of the Soul. It was written about in the Hebrew Bible when Jonah was swallowed by the whale. In some versions he gets consumed by the sea itself. Joseph Campbell describes how sometimes the hero gets lost in the dark woods. C. G. Jung called it being swallowed by the unconscious, by the shadow, a disintegration of the personality, what the alchemists called *nigredo*, the stage of the darkening of the soul prior to breakthrough. Arthur Koestler's book *The Act of Creation* gives a very good analysis. It examines this phenomenon through the lives of creative artists, thinkers, and the founders of religions, those who have gone through this night journey, this dissolution of self, as a means of bringing forth new ideas and insights to humanity. He argues this is how most new cultural forms are born.

At the time, I had no idea what pattern I was following. I was probably as clueless as that pupating worm. All I knew was that there was no way to stop it. It was like a wave crashing over me. There was no choice but to surrender.

One afternoon I woke, opened my eyes, and my sisters were there in the room, sitting next to my bed, visibly shocked by my condition. Perhaps they were coming to see me for the last time. Who knows, my wife may even have sent for them. It was written all over their faces that they thought I was dying. They were there to say goodbye to their beloved brother born with that birthmark on his arm, so full of promise, but who had obviously gone so badly wrong.

My wife was holding my head in her lap. My sons were there too, nobody knowing what to do. My wife was equally suffering with me, day by day, as if a piece of herself were dying.

In the middle of this scene, a cousin arrived from a distant village. He had no idea that I had been sick. When he saw me he couldn't help blurting out, "Oh, my God! What's happened to him? His hair has all gone white. He hardly seems to notice his surroundings. It looks as if he is dying!" Then he realized that my sisters had come to say goodbye, and that my wife was not only holding my head in her lap and stroking me, but that tears were running down her cheeks. When I realized this was my death vigil, I somehow mustered the energy to tell them that they should all go home now.

They must have thought I knew my time had come and that I wanted to die peacefully. My wife got up and walked them all to the door. Then she came back and embraced our sons. It was excruciating seeing them hanging on to each other as if they would now already have to face the world alone without me.

Hopelessly mismatched though my wife and I might have been, I have never felt as close to anybody in my life. She knew of my being with other women, but she also knew that I could never love anybody else. The others were just me playing out my passions, passing scenes on my very own personal path to Hell. It could have bothered her greatly. She could have grown bitter, but she didn't. On some level she knew better than I did what I had to go through. It showed great compassion and understanding, the way she accepted the odd course my life had taken, and still stood by me.

At our root we were one being. That is why I never told her, not once, "I love you." I've never said it to my sons either. To say *I love you* takes at its root that there are two beings, an I and a you. Here in the East we presuppose one being.

Chapter 23

Rebirth

Who knows how or why, maybe because my body was in such a state—the form was all but broken—but in the middle of that touching scene which could easily have been my last, my wife sitting across from me weeping, holding our two sons, my sisters having bid me adieu, it was at that dark moment that something happened that changed everything.

To say blinders were lifted from my eyes might sound trite, but since no words can possibly describe what happened, they might as well do. I was still there in the room. My wife and children were still weeping. Cars were still tooting their horns out on the street. The clock on the wall was still clicking out the seconds. The sun still inched across the sky, sending its brilliant rays in through the open window. Everything was just as it was. Nothing had changed—yet everything had changed. Things were just the way they were, yet they would never be the same.

My mind had stopped its commentary. It is that simple. There was experience and engagement with that experience, but there were no thoughts *about* that experience. Only experiencing. It was as if I had slipped through the crack between inside and outside, between the one experiencing and that which is experienced.

But let me stop speaking of the unspeakable right here. I've done enough damage already! If I say more, it would only confuse things further. My aim here is not to describe what did or did not occur that day but to place that experience within the context of my life. It is for this I have strayed into these dubious verbal waters.

Even if I were to keep it to a minimum and simply say that something happened, you might justifiably take me at my word. Yes, something happened—yet nothing happened; and this non-happening hit me like a thunderbolt. Like that, all my questions vanished. This answer to the riddle, if you want to call it that, was so simple, so self-evidently true, that I felt like hitting my forehead in wonder that it could have been staring me—and us all—in the face from the beginning, so well hidden in such plain sight. It had been right there, yet I had had to go so far, into such dangerous waters, to realize it.

Words cannot convey what I am talking about. They can only point, like a finger to the moon. Not that one can't use words. We *are* social beings. What would be more natural than to want to communicate this great and open secret? So you can play with words, employ paradox, speak in self-contradictory ways with the aim of tricking the mind out of its ruts.

For instance, when I say there was an experience that day, in fact there was no experience. That's why it might be more accurate to say that nothing happened! To say there was an experience would mean that something *happened*, and if something happened, if there was an experience, then there would have to have been a beginning, a middle, and an end, a before and an after to what we call the experience. This is how we experience things: they happen. Something occurs and we experience it. But this was different: in fact, it was as if for once nothing at all happened! For once there was *no* experience. Things remained as they were, in their original state. No beginning, no middle, no end.

Regardless of what I can and cannot say about this happening that did or did not occur, what I *can* describe is what happened to me on a physical level, for I felt it like a jolt, like a surge of energy. It entered my body. There is no other way to describe it. And at that moment I knew my descent was over, that I'd gotten what I came for, and that now I'd be coming back. This certainty came in an instant. I knew my strength would now return.

Somehow, I was able to convey this to my wife. I remember receiving this jolt of energy and concentrating my gaze upon my wife to communicate that the ordeal was over and that I'd be coming back. To this day, I don't know how I conveyed it, but by merely concentrating my gaze upon her she understood. And her tears of despair turned to tears of joy.

In the end, it is all a play of *tamasha*. *Tamasha* is a Punjabi word. It means a show, like a sideshow at a fair, maybe what Shakespeare meant when he said all the world is a stage and we are merely actors. But it happened like that. I then began to turn normality-wards, you could say. Normal, if you could say it is normal for a failed (or let us be charitable and say *former*) Sub-Divisional Officer with the Punjab Public Works Department, raised in a largely illiterate rural village, to be so audacious as to devote a dozen years to writing a book that earnestly proclaims to have uncovered the workings of the entire universe at all times, from the Big Bang on down!

I saw the gears spinning behind the obvious and received my insight in kernel form, like a seed with a spark within it. It took years of voracious and eclectic reading of everything from psychology and physics to history and philosophy for me to ground this vision, to give it flesh, and only twelve years later did I fully expel it from my system in the form of my book.

Perhaps it is difficult for you to grasp just how audacious it was of me to even think of writing a book. To the world I was either a failed district engineer or a saint gone bad, a misfit. I knew I had to base my exposition on more than my own ideas: thus my studies of everything from quantum physics and evolution to psychology—you name it. The teachings of Ramana Maharshi were invaluable. They helped me ground my experience.

I bought an electronic typewriter.

My father was living with us now. He was old and already considered me mad, a mad fool for having left my job without having an idea of what I was going to do. A square peg in a round hole: that's how he used to describe me.

But I didn't listen to him. I wasn't really there, but was being forced from inside to do what I did, researching and writing my book. I didn't care what others thought of me. I sat at my electronic typewriter (hardly anybody had even seen one in those days!) and I pecked out the first lines. I thought what the hell. I gave my book a title. I wrote it at the top of the first page: *A Grain of Truth*. I was sure that what I wrote would contain some basic ground, something foundational, that it would have some grain of truth, whether anybody would ever read it or understand it or not. My thought was that if in the end I was satisfied with it, I would maybe publish it myself, throw it into the world, and see what happens. I didn't bother about the reader. I didn't bother about a publisher.

Once I had the title at the top of the page, nothing happened, except a feeling of presumptuousness. Who was I to write a book? I was a nobody, a public works engineer of the Punjab government, Roads and Bridges, and a failed one at that, so mad as to resign his princely post to sit despondent at home, falling into a deathly mysterious illness, a descent into Hades, until it seemed the world was caving in around him.

My life had truly collapsed in on itself. It was like the gravitational collapse of a star that had expelled all its energy, becoming something resembling an enlarged sphere of burnt-out ash, which then, by dint of its own gravity, falls in on itself until what energy remains is concentrated in such an infinitesimally tiny point that it explodes, turning the wheel from contraction to expansion, a Big Bang, expanding from that tiny point into the entire of what we call the universe.

I thought, What's so great about your insight? So what if there are four fundamental forces and one's task is to free oneself from them? Isn't this basically the idea of all mystical traditions, that we come from the One, find ourselves in the many, entangled into this and that, and that our task, our longing, our destiny, is to ultimately free ourselves from the forces of this world?

There is a story, rather a joke, that goes something like this: Some property is stolen and people gather to discuss various schemes for catching the person who did it. Many ideas are bantered around until a little boy calls out, "I know who did it!" Everybody turns to him, full of expectation. And he exclaims, "It was a *thief!*"

I felt like that boy.

I was neither a scientist nor a philosopher. That is how I opened the book: I wrote that I am a nobody, but I have some devil in my mind, and I have to get rid of it. And actually, I think this is how religions are born, by someone who goes down so deep that he becomes dissolved, his own will and thoughts are exhausted, and then he can be used ('not my will, but thine')—if you get my meaning. They lose everything and then they come up with some very original thought. Jesus, Mohamad, Guru Nanak, even Buddha—they all went into some belly of the whale. This is actually just a symbolic way of saying it, to make others understand that they went deep, right to the bottom, dissolved, and were lost.

For me, the saving grace was that book based on my knowledge of the four forces. At my deepest point, beyond which I couldn't have gone without leaving my body, the point upon which I got stuck was that book. That is where I got caught, with the forces—my nemesis!

Now I can see that by going to the bottom I was enabled to have the experience, the insight, and that this insight saved me. And it has continued to be with me even up to this day. This book has been my life's work. Now, finally, I am no longer feeling tied to it—nor to this system. It is just that one gets entangled by trying to explain things intellectually, from the perspective of the ego. I never thought I would enter into the prison of the ego by trying to explain what came to me by experience, but somehow it had to happen. Entanglement and dis-entanglement. I wasn't yet forty and still had ground to plow. There were seeds to mature. I wasn't fully cooked. Still in my prime, I had work to do. This was my work. Perhaps I had fallen into the trap of the ego and thought I could express the inexpressible, use words for what they are inherently inadequately suited for.

Or perhaps the book was written for some other purpose, for the theory of the four forces to be expressed, no matter how imperfectly, even if you are the only one to date who has read the thing from cover to cover.

Einstein said we cannot know the fruit of our actions. I was pushed so hard from behind that I could not doubt the task that was before me. Maybe, like a plant that is allowed to enjoy the autumn with green leaves to the warming sun even after it has dropped its seeds and its 'purpose' has been realized, maybe I am now like that plant, my task (as I believed it at the time), my reason for being on this earth, was to write that book, and once written, now I am free again, and the book's fate is its own. It has nothing further to do with me. I gave it birth; that is all.

The main point was that science's attempt to unify the four forces, to understand the one behind the four, was doomed to fail.

Before reaching there, the very questioner will be absorbed into something greater and both the question and the questioner will be subsumed. It is like a moth attracted to the light of a candle with which it feels a longing to merge. It approaches, feels some heat, then turns back. It goes nearer, feels more heat, more longing to merge, and turns back. Later, after some time, at last, it prepares itself and is burnt. Once it merges with the light there is no one left. Words will definitely fail. There will be no one left behind to utter them!

Sometimes I feel like that, like I'm getting ever closer to the flame. I've told you that the doctors said I need surgery on my heart. Emergency surgery, they always say, and that it's a miracle I'm still alive. They've been saying this for the past five or seven years. But I've always refused. I've always known that the source of my bodily difficulties lies elsewhere. They say they have to bypass this and that, take veins from my legs—the whole thing. You've seen me: I never leave my rooms and the veranda. I only wash myself once a week. The effort leaves me breathless and with a pain in my chest.

CHAPTER 24

LIFE'S REVIEW

I didn't tell you when you came in this morning, but last night I almost died.

As I was falling asleep, I was going through all that I have told you, trying to see how I would sum it up, bring it to conclusion. Frankly, I was trying to make sense of it myself, this strange life I have led. Having told you my story in such detail, from beginning to end, it was all laid out fresh before my mind's eye. You could almost say I was attempting to see its purpose, if there be such a thing.

One lives one's life and memories follow; they collect over time. One recalls pieces, this and that situation, this stage in your life and that. But they tend to be isolated memories, like individual islands of the past, distinct memories triggered at different times for different reasons.

But now, thanks to our time together, the whole span of my life was laid out before me in all its rich detail. Never have I spoken as long as I have by telling you my story. And it was all in English! Since I am deaf, I tend, especially now in my elder years, towards a quiet life. And now that I am reaching the end of my story, naturally I turned to making sense of it all, putting it all together. What would I say to you as a means of summing it up, to bring it to conclusion? But really it was for myself that I was contemplating. What do *I* make of it, now that it has been laid out in all its graphic detail?

While my case may be extreme, man's existential situation is not that different. Each of us is stamped at birth and molded by our surroundings and the preexisting world into which we are born. Each one of us finds him- or herself in a particular set of circumstances over which he or she has no apparent say—who your parents are, which nation and neighborhood you were born into, which moment in history into which you were thrown.

We awaken to the fact that we are already entered into a flow of something greater than ourselves, apart from which we do not—and cannot—exist. We wake up to find ourselves already embedded, already bound; we awaken to the fact that we are already entangled. We are each of us in a knot of entangled circumstance which, to a remarkable degree, confines us and defines who and what we are.

Unique as we are as individuals, so it is that each knot is unique. The goal, the riddle, for each of us is to untie his or her own knot. No one else can do it for us. That alone is each of our unique work. Another man could have done my engineering job overseeing the construction of roads and dams and bridges. The crew might not have had as much fun doing it, but the work would probably have gotten done. The only work on this earth that can definitely only be done by me is that of unraveling the conundrum of my own being. That is my real job, as it is for you. All jobs that we take on for pay are ultimately to feed our bellies while we do this other work.

The trick is really detachment. Perhaps detachment isn't the right word—and there might not be a right word. Again words fail. What I mean by detachment has nothing to do with being aloof, cold, and the like. By being detached I mean the actor has some degree of awareness that he is but an actor on a stage, that this is all a *tamasha*, a big show. Which is not to say he is less passionately playing out his part, or less caring. He might still take it seriously, but in a different way. With this awareness comes freedom, and the spark of spontaneity.

A nighttime equivalent, an analogy to what I mean here by detachment, would be to realize while dreaming that you are in a dream. To do this, one must withdraw one's identification with the dreamer, with the I of the dream. Haven't you ever pulled yourself out of a dream, especially when a dream goes sour or you suddenly find yourself about to be caught by some ogre or be overcome by some other calamity? Haven't you ever woken yourself up out of a dream with the increasingly conscious realization that what you're experiencing is only a dream, and that really you are lying in your bed with your head on a pillow? Maybe it is a beautiful dream and you try to fall back asleep, half-aware you are 'only' dreaming, hoping it will continue. Regardless, this is the detachment of which I speak: the wedge between the witness and that which he is witnessing, between the actor and his or her part. It is also to wake up to the dreamlike quality of this life.

The word *detachment* comes from a French word that also means to untie. So by detach I also mean to untie yourself from your entanglements, to make space between you as witness and the one who is playing his part. This requires an increase of consciousness, a wider perspective. You become conscious of something you weren't conscious of before. With the rise in consciousness, the solution to your problem might also transform. Like in the dream of the ogre chasing you. From within the dream the solution might be to find a place to hide or to find a stick with which to fight back. But from the wider perspective, the real solution is to wake up!

What I am talking about is disentangling, not from the world, but from one's attachment and identification with it—to be in the world but not of it, as they say. Maybe the Buddhists call this realizing emptiness. Detached, you will be traveling light. You might even make it through the eye of the needle.

As I lay on my bed last night I thought about my book, and how my insight into the four forces had brought me back from the brink all those years ago, how I'd taken twelve years to write that book, how I've held onto it since.

Then I felt a sudden release, as if I could drop it now. I've always thought it must contain at least a grain of truth, and I've held onto that. But now, while lying in bed, flat on my back looking up into the darkened room, in that silence and complete darkness, my life laid out before me as a result of our meetings, I felt ready, for the first time, to relinquish even that, to let my book and my theory of the four forces go.

I came here to this house in the hills this monsoon to leave everything behind: my life in the Punjab, my family, to leave all of that—at least for a few months. I was expecting to live in silence and without need, to speak with no one but the caretaker and his wife, who have been providing me with food. And then there you were, living upstairs, a writer, and before I knew it we were embarked on this journey of my telling you my story.

And now I have told it. As I said, I was lying in my bed in the darkness and it was all laid out before my mind's eye, clear as day.

It was then that something happened. Something fell from me. It felt as if the last piece of my worldly ambition popped like that balloon that ceased to be all those years ago with my initial experience. It simply ceased to be. I was enveloped in the most wonderful silence, and I knew my work was now done. I had told my story, and now it was complete.

I couldn't help thinking about Lao Tzu, the ancient Taoist philosopher. He, too, had been involved in words as the keeper of the archives at the royal court. Then, one day, when he was in advanced age, he left it all behind. He went to the gate at the western edge of the great Chinese kingdom, somewhere on the border of the wilds of Tibet and the Western Mountains.

When he was about to pass through, he was stopped by the gatekeeper who sensed he was not an ordinary man. He asked the old man why he wanted to pass through and where he was going. Lao Tzu said he wanted to retire from the world and disappear from it.

The gatekeeper, seeing that he was a man of unusual insight and learning, and that he had once held a high position with the emperor, was nervous about letting him pass through the gate and disappear into the wilderness beyond. He made Lao Tzu write his wisdom down into a short book, at the completion of which he let Lao Tzu pass. This is how Lao Tzu's *Tao Te Ching* came into existence. It has been with us for over 2,500 years. Lao Tzu was never heard from again.

As I lay there in the darkness, I had to laugh at you playing the part of the gatekeeper and my playing Lao Tzu. My work was not only complete, but the story told. It was now up to you what to do with it.

I was free to pass on.

It was with this happy thought that I fell asleep.

CHAPTER 25

THE LAST NIGHT?

The next thing I knew—it must have been two or three in the morning—I woke up gasping for breath. A tremendous weight, like an elephant, was sitting on my chest. I was lying on my back in the darkness, and the breath wasn't coming to me. I thought maybe this was it, this would be my last night. Completed, or as we say in Punjabi, *poora hogia.*

Many times I've been prepared to die. Almost half my life. And I've always felt entirely alright with it. I thought OK, let us go! Let's finally see what happens. Why not? It will happen sooner or later. But as you can see, I didn't go. Last night's incident ended as it always has—so far: the story didn't end. I'm still here. I lay like that on my back—preparing and prepared—for two, three, four hours, until the break of day.

Did you hear the storm that came through last night, the almost continuous lightning, the thunder that roared without end? Well, a storm came through last night and got stuck on the mountains. Just before daybreak it rolled back down the valley and away. And as it departed it took with it that pain in my chest. It dissipated with the retreating thunder.

I am now well over seventy years of age. So it is OK. I am ready to go. When you have a seven on the left side of your age, I feel it is honorable. You are not going early. Now I have told you about my life. Maybe you will write the book, maybe not. Maybe I will live to see it—maybe not.

It doesn't matter.

Things will end in whatever way. All things end. All this philosophy, these ideas, the four forces—all these things end. And in the end you feel as if you've been dreaming some kind of dream.

Much can be learned from this thing called dream. Dreams are just like life: they are spontaneous. They happen automatically. Yet when we are dreaming we are unaware that we are lying with our head on a pillow with feet that are either hot or cold! We find ourselves there, in our dreams, unaware that we are dreaming.

Before dreaming, we must first fall asleep. And falling asleep is not that different from what the mystics mean by waking up, what they call enlightenment. I would call it a quantum jump. In either case, you can't give anyone much useful advice, perhaps other than just to relax. There can be no system to teach you how to fall asleep, no more than one can teach anything useful to make one wake up to the perspective of the One. If there was a system, say a twelve-step program, to teach you how to sleep, you'd have to forget it entirely—let it go along with all other thoughts—upon reaching the very threshold of sleep. Ultimately, it would be useless to you. And if you thought about it too much you might never fall asleep. You'd think about it till the break of day! Yes, too much thought about sleep, just like too much thought about becoming enlightened, would keep you from it. To sleep, you must let your mind drift from the here and now of sensory experience. Sleep happens while you are not aware. Who actually remembers falling asleep? We wake up, and only then do we realize that we were sleeping, and surmise, therefore, that we must have fallen asleep.

Yes, waking up, piercing through to that state of oneness, to what is called the Understanding, the knowledge of the Atma as we say in India, what the Buddhists call Enlightenment, whatever label you put on it—it is not that different from our nightly occurrence of falling asleep.

Psychologists say dreams are useful for resolving problems and fulfilling wishes, and whatever else lies lodged deeply within us. Similarly, on the greater level, so is this life, or so it seems: it is as if we were sent here to resolve that which needs resolving.

The wise ones speak in riddles. They say that there was no creation, and that there will be no destruction. They give us paradox. You were born of a barren mother, they say. No path, no achievement. You sort of awaken from the dream. You laugh at your whole philosophy, the whole construct of mind—you laugh at it.

Like my grand theory that I spent twelve years expounding. Thanks to our encounter, I feel ready now, as if I'm ready to let it go: true or not true, it is also but a play, a *tamasha*. Even if that book was written not for the present age, blinded as it is by the successes of the rational mind. Even if the book was really written for a distant future age, and someone from that distant future will read the book and know that someone back then, back in those dark ages of unalloyed rational thought, understood the limitations of his own age. Still, it seems proper to me that I transcend the book and leave it all behind. I could not have done this earlier, even though I went to hell and back again to gain the insights contained in it—even though I've clung to it ever since. It is time for me to enter a new phase. The book has fulfilled its function. It was like a life raft for me, the four planks of which were the four forces and the universe reflected in them. It brought me back to the surface, gave me reason for being, gave answers to the questions that haunted me, especially when it came to the purpose of my being.

In reality, I have nothing to say. I have nothing to say and you have nothing to hear. We have simply come into contact with each other. I had a story. You were a writer seeking a story. Now I have told you my memories. I say this was my life. But memories are like a dream, making coherence out of the chaos of experience. Memories filter the lived reality. Now what I have told you will work through your memory, your filtering system, and you will write a book, maybe. The *tamasha* continues. The play. All is a *tamasha*. Nothing serious in it. It began a few years before, and it will end a few years hence.

In India, there is another word for *tamasha*: *lila*. It also means a play, but it is more of a religious word. *Lila* is what they call the creator god Brahma's play, the play of some god creating the world in which we are all apparently participating. This is how the Hindus speak of it. So if you are of a religious bent of mind you can call it *lila*, a divine play. If not, you can do like Shakespeare and just call it a play acted on the stage we call the world. It is up to you. For myself, being neither religious nor non-religious, I call it a *tamasha* going on, like a sideshow at a fair, and it is quite funny. You can also call it a house of suffering, like Buddha did. But it is also a house of enjoyment. It contains everything.

We human beings are put into a situation. We try to understand it, to describe it, to bind it with our words. We bind everything with our words. We have named everything. When you name something, you separate it from its background. You make a distinction. You say it is this and not that. We can only think of one thing at a time. We put it into the sequence. Maybe we even put it into spacetime itself so that we can understand it. Maybe otherwise there would be no spacetime.

It is by entering our sphere of spacetime that the thought can arise. To be experienced is to be experienced in time. From what do thoughts arise? Where are our thoughts prior to our having them? Where do thoughts go after we have had them? Surely, they are no longer bound by any spacetime. It appears that it is to give space and time to experience that there arises what we call space, what we call time.

All I can really say is be yourself. Life is neither a plus nor a minus—neither a bed of roses nor a crown of thorns. It has some pluses and some minuses, some enjoyment and some pains and suffering. Find your own place in the scheme of things and live accordingly.

First, understand this world to the best of your ability, up to the limit of your knowing facility. Penetrate it with your heart. Penetrate its meaning as best you can, and let that be your guide—that is all. That's how it's been for me, how I've been doing it. Right or wrong, nobody can say—and perhaps there is no right or wrong. Know yourself, then act accordingly. This is my philosophy.

Just as there are different parts of a tree—the root, the trunk, the bark, the branches, the twigs, the flower buds and the fruit— so it is that there are people existing on many different levels, some high, some low. Each is serving his or her purpose, just as there are roots and trunks and branches and little twigs. Isn't it often upon the smallest twig that ultimately grows the fruit? Just as all parts of the tree are needed, so are all levels of understanding. All things are interwoven. Which part of the tree can we say is right or wrong?

He who will come to know himself will know himself. Why should he listen to me! Does the bud need coaching to become a flower? What if I were to say to everyone, 'Just be yourself. Relax!' What would I really be teaching? There cannot be one rule for all. Everybody is unique. Maybe it is better if someone comes to you and asks some earnest question that you give some spontaneous answer, even if you contradict it a moment later. That may be the teaching for him, of the moment—maybe not. There are no rules for all. William Blake wrote somewhere, "One law for the lion and the ox is oppression." Ramana Maharshi said, "Do what is right at a given moment and leave it behind." If I tell you to act with equanimity and calm when actually the next stage in your evolution demands that you fight, that you live through your passions, then won't I be teaching a lion to become a vegetarian? In reality, to perfect something in the perfect scheme of things, one need not even speak. No teaching—nothing. Just be yourself. And do whatever you want to do. That is all. As it says in your Bible, there is a time for *every* purpose under Heaven, a time to love—and a time to hate! There is even a time to open your mouth, and a time to keep it shut!

From the outside we all may look like brothers and sisters of a single species, but for human beings the difference really lies within. From their mind one is a lion, one a fox, another is a hen. So to really see the differences in human beings you must know their mind. And you will see that they are also like these animals. From the outside you can tell a lion from a jackal. You can't do this with humans.

Better a bad man acting badly, showing who he is to the world, than one of these goody-goodies who looks so pious and squeaky-clean from the outside, but hides who he really is within. At least the man we call a bad man is being honest. There is coherence between his being and his actions. By being authentic, by acting from who he really is, even if he acts like a rogue, he is bound to be in a better position to further his evolution than the man who plays by the rules but hides his true thoughts.

That is how I see it.

Our lessons come naturally, and nature's punishment always fits the crime. When you are a child and you fall, you skin your knee. This helps teach you how to overcome falling. It teaches you to stand with confidence on your own two feet.

I'd rather be in the company of a thief than a saint. Babas, no matter how they start their careers, if they are successful they usually succumb to their followers' and society's expectations of how a saint is supposed to behave. That's also why I resisted becoming a saint. I didn't want to be one of those god-men who hide the bottle from public view and drink secretly. If I want a drink, I'll not hide it. And if I drank, that would confuse my followers. It wouldn't fit their image of a saint, and they would leave me anyway.

I'd rather be spontaneous and without followers, leaving people wondering whether I am a saint or a thief, free to act this way one moment and that way the next, and live in obscurity. Above all, I want to be free.

By being yourself you will be helping others, and by helping others you will be helping yourself. Think of the rose. It has not made that smell in order to please anyone. It has just grown to its potential. What it has to give automatically goes to the other. So at the end of the day, if you do something for someone it is best to forget it. Besides, it is only on the surface that you do something for someone else. And if you think it was you who did the deed, you will think of repayment, as if something is now owed to you. This usually creates problems.

See how nature, or the scheme of things, has helped you to cross over some very difficult times. There is a tendency, a pull, an almost magnetic attraction towards unraveling the knot and binding us back with the One. So you could say my philosophy is a positive one.

Rest assured that nature has her methods and nature will assist you. You will not be left alone. My one and only belief is that she is binding us back to her bosom—to the extent that we don't get in the way, which is a tall order given the strength of the ego. Rather than depend on any person, depend upon the natural scheme of things, the natural unfoldment. Then you have no need to worry. You will realize that you needn't *do* anything. You will see that everything is happening on its own.

There are many babas, many gurus, many teachers, mystics, fakirs who talk as if they will give you the experience or you will get the experience by being in their presence, by doing what they say, by following their path. Religions also tell you to follow their path in order to reach some sort of level.

One day, Ramana Maharshi, the great modern sage of South India, was having his legs massaged by some of his disciples. He abruptly brushed their hands away and started massaging his legs himself. The disciples felt rebuked, as if they weren't doing a good job. One of them gathered his courage and asked the master why he had pushed them away. Ramana said, laughing, "You think by massaging my legs you will gain some merit and get something from God? Why shouldn't I get this benefit myself?"

Another time someone came to Ramana and asked him, "What should I do to attain the Understanding?" Ramana said, "Do whatever you were doing. Live the way you are living. Go the way you came."

I see it rather that when the individual is ripe, he would have had the experience anyway. Anything could be the trigger. There was another great sage in twentieth century India, Vivekananda, who merely touched the foot of his teacher Ramakrishna and went into profound *samadhi*, a state of total absorption with the One.

People say this proves the power of Ramakrishna, as if a current moved through him and endowed the mystic experience upon Vivekananda. Even if something did happen there—say an exchange of some sort of high frequency energy—Vivekananda must still have been ready for it. No doubt many touched the feet of such a revered teacher as Ramakrishna. But the others didn't enter *samadhi*. Vivekananda was ripe. That's the important thing: he was ripe and it happened. Ramakrishna didn't give him the experience. One can say he had the experience because he was ripe, and being ripe it just happened on its own—like a bud that suddenly comes to flower. It could have come through anything—even through the touch of a girl. It could have been by seeing a sunset, or the rising sun strike a Himalayan peak. Anything could have been the trigger. Important is that it was inside him, there in his being. He was prepared. What he then touched is not important.

We may talk of these matters, what people call 'spiritual' experience. We can speak about it and we can enjoy speaking about it, but if you expect it to get you somewhere, we might as well be talking about the weather. Nothing from the outside can ever give you the experience. No one can bestow it upon you. Nor can we really talk much of the experience, except to say it is something like that love at first sight, when one feels a merging with something greater.

People everywhere enjoy speaking of love—especially young people. Yet if you speak of that oceanic moment of love at first sight with someone who has never experienced it, you might enjoy yourself speaking of it and the other may enjoy hearing about it. But nothing of what you say will have any bearing on whether that other person will ever have that experience of love at first sight. Still, people do it all the time: they talk about love. They have fun exchanging stories. And so it is that we can enjoy talking about these 'spiritual' matters, but it doesn't mean much. We can talk about it just to enjoy ourselves, just to pass the time.

But there comes a time when even this kind of talk becomes superfluous, when the longing arises to communicate no more with our fellow human beings, to go like Lao Tzu, who simply disappeared into the Western Mountains and was heard from no more—except for the echoes of his passing which have been resounding in legend for 2,500 years.

Maybe you could call this blissful state Second Childhood, when one returns, transformed, to the completeness and wonder that was ours at birth. Gone is the feeling of being alone in the jungle and having to call out, for we have discovered something and we are satisfied. It comes with the realization of what I am, and that I am no different from the other. I am. I am what I am. I am what this is. I am also what that is. And so I am not lost.

Something has happened to me in the course of our encounters. It culminated last night as I lay with that pain in my chest. It has been dawning within me: the end of my need to communicate my story and understanding to others. I will soon reach the point where I will have no need of words, and slowly, as if retracing the course of a baby back to before it learned to speak, I will go beyond words. Who knows, if we meet again after some years I may not speak—not even a word. What have I to say? First, I will not teach. Nobody can teach these things to another person. Therefore, I have nothing to give.

The real benefit of understanding is that the understanding itself is likeable; it is enjoyable. We are what we are. We are Shiva and Parvati in one! Energy and form. If I were to have one, this would be my final point: What is the Understanding if it doesn't bring you happiness?

No words can express the perspective of the One. Poetry tries. Paradox, which has been resorted to by masters of both Sufi and Zen schools for hundreds of years, sometimes works. Paradox has long been utilized by those trying to convey what can only come in through the cracks *between* the words. Getting stuck on the words is like the dog's fixation on the tip of his master's finger and missing the moon.

No matter what you say, if you make an assertion about something you are saying it is like this and not like that. You are dividing the world into what this thing is and everything else. That is what makes speaking and words so odious. You begin with division, dividing the world into this and that. Then you define what this is by what sets it apart from that. That's why if, following in the footsteps of some of the great sages of India, you say you are not the doer of your actions, that things are simply happening through you, it is all just happening, it is all God's will—however you want to express it—if you say anything at all on the subject, you will always be doomed to failure and you will hopelessly miss the mark. This is to be accepted as a condition of opening one's mouth. It is simply the way it is. This is our human condition.

Those who promise to show the way and have something to say naturally gather followers. Lost souls that we are, we long for the wise man or woman, the one who can enlighten us. This is how babas become babas, gurus gurus, and all the rest of it, even saviors: it is their bread and butter, how they make their living, you could say. It is their role in the world. They have something to teach to make you a better person. But in the process they tend to forget that this is all a dream, and that one day we might just wake up!

A *tamasha* can be imbedded within another *tamasha*, like a dream within a dream. It is like an onion—like the atom itself:

peel off its layers and look for something solid, resembling matter as we experience it, and you will not find it.

I could have become a baba. It would have been far easier if I had, my path of least resistance. But I fought it. My whole life I've tried to kill the baba, the saint, that which they wanted to make of me. Yet that mark on my skin, that black stain, applied pressure. Because of it I had to ask those questions; I had to press further than the common man. It has hounded me my entire life, this question of my babahood. It's been like a fire in my ass.

And whatever you think of this birthmark—this stamp—upon my arm, whether you think it means I am an incarnation of that saint, or even his son (I was born nine months after his death so it isn't entirely out of the question), whether, as your Western scientist might conclude after a thorough examination, it was a random mutation of some gene, or even whether it was a bad joke played upon me by some dreaming god with a strange sense of humor, still one cannot deny that it has marked me for life.

So please excuse me if over the course of our time together I have given in to temptation and wagged my tongue a little too freely and given a bad imitation of a sage. If someone comes and puts me a saint-like question and talks to me as if I'm a saint, I may reply like a saint. If a thief comes and speaks to me as one thief talks to another, I may talk with him like a thief. If you ask me suspicious questions, you'll probably find things to be suspicious about. Speak to me like a child, and I'll become like a child. I might even talk nonsense! It only proves that I am still like that jungle man, just wanting to call out, hoping for a reply. Yet I think our encounter has cured me of it: I am ready to speak no more.

Live your life; that's all you have to do. If you just live your life, you will be serving nature's purpose directly. You need do nothing special. Do whatever you were doing. Like Ramana said, go the way you came. Just be yourself and live your life. It is a great release when you realize there is nothing to be done—nothing to be obtained, nothing lost. You need change nothing. It is enough just to be. Being is enough. Everything is in its place. Be true to yourself. Find your own self, then act accordingly. If you feel like loving, love. If you feel like hating, hate.

This advice is so simple that it may never catch on general-ly. Probably because how would you sell it? Isn't it true that the bestselling books in the West usually contain the twelve steps to becoming this or that better person? How is a baba to survive if he has no technique, no magic influence to convey, if he simply echoes Socrates' basic counsel to 'Know Thyself' and leaves it at that. With nothing to sell, who's going to buy it? Who would fol-low the saint that performs no miracles? And what are miracles anyway? As Einstein said, "There are only two ways to live your life: as though nothing is a miracle, or as though everything is a miracle."

My telling you my story: it is as if I had a dream, and then I told you about it. Your writing this, perhaps, one day will also be a dream. And the person reading this. And then some day you might wake up only to find there was no dream, there was no world, there was no life. There was nothing. It was all just writ-ing on water.

Whatever you write, or don't write, about what I've told you—it is up to you. My only request is that you tell it not in a scandalous way, in a way that will offend the common man or shed ill light on my family members. This could cause me trouble.

My other request is that if you do write the book you don't use my real name. It might give people the wrong impression. They might try to find me. They may try to turn me into a baba yet! Your book could become well known. Who knows what is in the scheme of things? If people knew my name, maybe they would give me no peace—thinking I had something to say!

Epilogue

It is the middle of the night and Vikram's story is reverberating through my mind. I am lying upstairs in bed, listening to the rain pelt the slate roof. Yet another monsoon thunderhead has come lumbering up the valley and stalled against the high mountains, dropping an endless torrent of heavy, lashing rain. Here in the Himalayan foothills the land is so steeply sloped that it easily sheds quantities of water that elsewhere would cause flash floods.

The bedroom is illuminated by bright flashes of lightning. The rumble of thunder renewing itself continuously and echoing off the surrounding mountains is punctuated by sharp claps right overhead. It has been like this since I woke up well over an hour ago. Barbara is next to me, sweetly sleeping. It is late in the monsoon, and these storms don't usually wake us.

I, too, would be sleeping, but I am thinking of Vikram. We have been meeting almost daily for weeks now, untold hours immersed in what, because of his deafness, has amounted to an almost unbroken monologue. It was just twenty-four hours ago, in a storm he described as very much like this one, that Vikram lay with a sharp pain in his chest like a ton weight—with the breath, as he said, not coming to him.

As I lie staring into the flashing darkness, I imagine him just downstairs, where he must also be lying in bed, perhaps staring into the flashing darkness, as he had the night before. Could his heart right now again be malfunctioning?

He had spoken of that original use of language, to tell the other, "I am here." Yet if he called out now there would be no one to hear him. Could it be, now that he had bequeathed me the story of his sojourn on this planet, that he was now free to go, that he was, as he said, moving beyond words? Would it really be unreasonable to imagine that at this very moment something dramatic could be happening downstairs?

If anyone else I cared about had told me of a night such as he'd had last night with the sharp pain in his chest and inability to breathe, I would have done something. Maybe I would have fetched a doctor, brought some medicine, or made sure someone was within earshot should he call out for help. I would have checked on him from time to time.

But I had done nothing of the sort.

Such was the spell he cast upon me by speaking of the great *tamasha*—the play of time and space unfolding as human experience, with no greater importance than that of a sideshow at a fair.

No doubt more details could be told of this or that period of his life. His ideas and philosophy could always be cloaked in other words, revealing other facets. There would always be more to tell. We could no doubt go on for days or even longer with our daily sessions.

Yet it could also end here.

Lying awake in the flashing darkness, I feel unsettled. My imagination keeps running away with me, taking me through different possible scenarios. It is not easy to control my wild fantasies. Every time I find myself imagining what it would be like to find him dead in the morning, I remind myself that it would be too much like the resounding final scene from a piece of fiction. It is by remembering this that I am able to cool myself off, by convincing myself that my imagination has once again gone wild. After all, this heart problem has been with him for years. He told me of many such episodes. Yet he had lain in bed just the night before with what, according to his description, could very well have been a heart attack.

Never have I encountered anyone who treated death with such nonchalance. It was sometimes disquieting, even unnerving. It revealed the level of acceptance he had achieved in his life. He would no doubt greet death with the same enthusiasm and passion he greeted other things.

Vikram told me he had spent the first half of his life preparing, and the second half prepared, to die. He had had many close calls, which he'd always brushed off as mere byproducts of a much more important process.

Yet now that he has told me his life story, and knowing what doing so has meant for him, what it means for his own evolution, I can't help coming back to the feeling that probably for the first time he is traveling light enough to glide safely beyond all that entangles the rest of us.

It has become increasingly clear that the seeming coincidence of his moving in downstairs and my recording his story has had an important function for him, without which he would not now be ready. It seems natural that this could be his time to pass to that place beyond words.

Our last session, heightened by his close brush with death, demonstrated that he was ready. Like Lao Tzu, who had to leave behind a book before he could pass through the gate to the Western Mountains, Vikram has left me with his story. Having lived his life and having left a record, couldn't it be, even by his own estimation, that he has now exhausted what he was here for?

How not to toy with the fantasy that he has now, as they say in Punjabi, "completed," except by reminding myself once again that such an ending was only found in fiction. Yet with a life stamped as it was from birth, with so many unusual and meaningful twists that couldn't be made up, how not to lie in that flashing darkness, the silence broken by tremendous thunderous roars echoing off the mountains, and entertain the possibility that in the morning I might make a momentous discovery.

Shortly before sunrise, the storm lets up and rolls back down the valley as Vikram described it had last night, leaving behind a feeling of peace. I lie awake until the sun starts streaming into our bedroom's eastern window.

I don't tell Barbara of my fitful night. I suppose I don't want to lend the premonition credence by voicing it. At about nine I take the almost-empty compost bucket and, even though the sky is darkening and the next thunderhead is closing in on us and it is beginning to gust and rain, I tell Barbara I am going to the compost pile. She doesn't think anything of it.

I bound down those steep stairs, and when I get to Vikram's

veranda I am met with a cold wet gale. The wooden door to Vikram's rooms is open and the screen door unlatched. It is flapping in the wind. They say wind is the soul itself, is life, is breath. Like the open door of a birdcage—has this bird taken wing?

I burst inside the front room, where we had sat all those hours together, and go straight through the open door to his bedroom.

It takes a moment of stunned silence for me to realize that the room is empty of his things and that he is not there. His bag and few possessions are all gone. I stumble back into the front room and realize that it, too, is bare of his possessions, of any sign of his ever having been there.

He is gone.

I drop myself into the chair I know so well in front of the little round table and look at his empty chair, the chair in which he had spent so many hours speaking of his life and ideas, his hands never at rest.

I sit there in silence for so long that Barbara comes down looking for me, wondering if I've gotten lost.

ACKNOWLEDGEMENTS

I would like to thank the original Vikram, for his story.

Just as a mirror is needed for us to see our own faces, a writer needs good readers, and I would like to thank the following people for reading the manuscript for this book in its various drafts. Their help is greatly appreciated and had a hand in making this book, such as it is, what it is: Alice Karow, David Michie, David Rodgers, Dylan Lott, Eli Jellenc, Ian Baker, Joao Ferrira, Kim Parker, Regina Franke, Robyn Whatley-Kahn, and Steve Brock. Special thanks to Alice Karow for book design ideas. And extra special thanks go to Barbara for ideas, suggestions, edits, and beautiful companionship all along the way.

ABOUT THE AUTHOR

Writer and photographer Thomas K. Shor was born in Boston, USA, and studied comparative religion and literature in Vermont. With an ear for unusual stories, the fortune to attract them, and an eye for detail, he has travelled the planet's mountainous realms—from the Mayan Highlands of southern Mexico in the midst of insurrection to the mountains of Greece, and more recently, to the Indian Himalayas—to collect, illustrate, and write stories with a uniquely personal character, often having the flavour of fable.

Shor has lectured widely on his writings and has had solo exhibits of his photographs in Europe and India. He can often be found in the most obscure locales, immersed in a compelling story touching upon fundamental human themes.

Visit him at www.ThomasShor.com

ALSO BY THOMAS K. SHOR

A STEP AWAY FROM PARADISE

THE TRUE STORY OF A TIBETAN LAMA'S JOURNEY TO A LAND OF IMMORTALITY

PENGUIN BOOKS, 2011
CITY LION PRESS, 2017
AUDIBLE AUDIOBOOK, 2019

IN THE EARLY 1960s, a Tibetan lama, a charismatic and learned visionary mystic named Tulshuk Lingpa, led over 300 followers into the high glaciers of the Himalayas in order to 'open the way' to a hidden land of immortality fabled in Tibetan tradition dating back at least to the 12th century.

Fifty years later, Thomas K. Shor tracks down the surviving members of this visionary expedition and entwines their remarkable stories of faith and adventure with his own quest to discover the reality of this land known as Beyul. What emerges is a breathtaking story

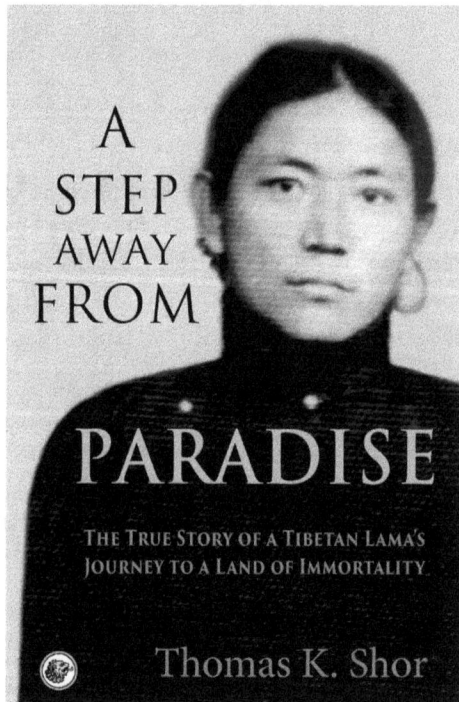

alive with possibility, bringing the reader as close to the Hidden Land as a book possibly can. As the astounding account unfolds, the reader is sure to repeat the question constantly raised by the author in his interviews: And then what happened?

A STEP AWAY FROM PARADISE tells the story of Lama Tulshuk Lingpa's life and his unlikely expedition to a land beyond cares while reflecting on what this means for the rest of us. It draws on both research and extensive interviews with his surviving disciples and family members. The book is richly illustrated with portraits of those who went with Tulshuk Lingpa and the places he traveled to. The book also delves into the tradition within Tibetan Buddhism of Shambhala and the hidden valleys, which mirror legends around the world of utopias and lands of milk and honey, thus showing that the quest for the hidden land is a universal urge of humanity.

FROM THE FOREWORD BY
JETSUNMA TENZIN PALMO

A STEP AWAY FROM PARADISE is a riveting tale of adventure, intrigue and Devotion. [It] deals with an aspect of Tibetan Buddhism that is in some ways more honest to the real spirit of Tibet than all the usual books on Tibetan doctrine and will, I am sure, be of interest to a wide audience. It is a fascinating account of a little-known charismatic figure that will challenge even the most skeptical mind and provide a fresh perspective on what we normally regard as 'reality.'

Like no other book I have ever read, A STEP AWAY FROM PARADISE is both unique and intriguing. Highly recommended.

INTO THE HANDS OF THE UNKNOWN

AN INDIAN SOJOURN WITH A HARVARD RENUNCIANT

Escape Media Publishers, 2003
Pilgrim Publishers, 2006
City Lion Press, 2019

"I think you should come with me to India"

Thus begins the story of the author at the age of 21, when he happened to sit next to Ed Spencer, a brilliant 70-year-old ex-Harvard professor turned wandering holy man, who makes this offer within an hour of their meeting on a Greek ferry.

Though unsure whether the old man is some kind of a bum or a realized being or both, he agrees to go with this enigmatic stranger whose credo is: "Take the money out of your pocket and put yourself in the hands of the Unknown."

When they arrive at the border and Ed passes the money exchange with hardly a glance, Shor begins to understand the gulf that separates the old man from the rest of humanity.

The ensuing journey takes us on an epic trip by foot into the heart of South India and then to the Himalayas where the author makes his first contact with the Tibetan people.

INTO THE HANDS OF THE UNKNOWN has been revised and has a new Postscript describing Shor's subsequent encounters with Ed Spencer. The book was originally published as Part II of WINDBLOWN CLOUDS.

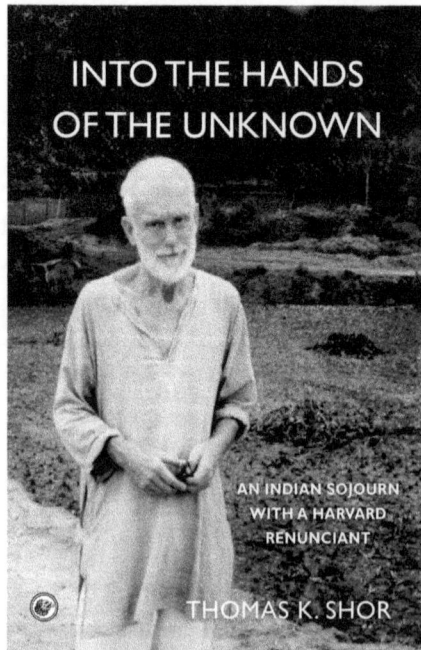

INTO THE HANDS OF THE UNKNOWN

AN INDIAN SOJOURN WITH A HARVARD RENUNCIANT

THOMAS K. SHOR

THE MASTER DIRECTOR
A Journey through Politics, Doubt and Devotion with a Himalayan Master

HarperCollins, 2014
City Lion Press, 2019

"Maybe you shouldn't go back to Darjeeling. It might not be safe for you..."

The lama was in the next room. It was 2 a.m. He was trying to calm his attendants. I think the boys wanted to kill me.

This was my last day with Gurudev.

In this riveting true story, Thomas K. Shor, an adventuring American writer with an ear for unusual stories, has no idea what he is getting into when he wanders into a Sikkimese mountain village and into the life of an enigmatic spiritual master known as Gurudev.

As Gurudev, a Tibetan Buddhist lama, lavishes the author with presents and invites him into his inner circle—thereby offering him, and us, a unique glimpse into a master's life and his teachings of universal love—it seems destiny is at work. But what happens when it turns out the master has close ties with the local dictator and his henchmen and Shor finds himself staying with the lama at their houses? How is he to reconcile the religion of love with the violence of politics? Gurudev's 'engaged Buddhism' not only stretches common notions of morality, but also spins Shor's moral compass. Ultimately, the author flees Darjeeling under physical threat and abandons the writing of this book—until now.

THE MASTER DIRECTOR, richly illustrated with over 75 photos, probes the limits of charisma and skepticism, doubt, and devotion. And throughout, Shor's captivating story treads the fine line of openness without credulity, and questioning without prejudice. While the warnings are many against mixing religion and politics, they combine in this entertaining tale set in the politically tumultuous foothills of India's eastern Himalayas to reveal profound insights into the nature of both the human and the divine.

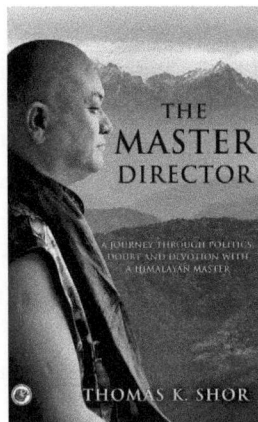

THE MONK AND THE SLY CHICKPEA

TRAVELS ON CORFU

Escape Media Publishers, 2003
City Lion Press, 2019

THE MONK AND THE SLY CHICKPEA tells the story of a journey the author took in 1981 as a young man to the Greek island of Corfu. His journey starts in an idyllic coastal village in a house surrounded by lush fruit and olive trees. While many a young man's journey to Greece would feature a coastal village and even a strip of white beach, Shor's journey led him, with a certain inevitability, to the island's highest mountain, the wind-swept and craggy Mount Pantokrator, and to the ancient stone monastery that crowns its peak. It was there that he lived with the monastery's sole inhabitant of over forty years, the fiery-eyed Greek Orthodox monk Evthókimos Koskinás, a man of both the mountain and of God. From that stormy peak, often pounded by bolder-splitting lightning, sharing meals of chickpeas seasoned with the mountain's wild herbs drenched in olive oil, Shor comes to some startlingly profound insights for a young man of twenty-two.

THE MONK AND THE SLY CHICKPEA, which is revised and has a new Postscript describing the author's return to Corfu and his encounters with the monk after twenty years, was originally published as Part I of the book *WINDBLOWN CLOUDS* by Escape Media Publishers, USA, in 2003.

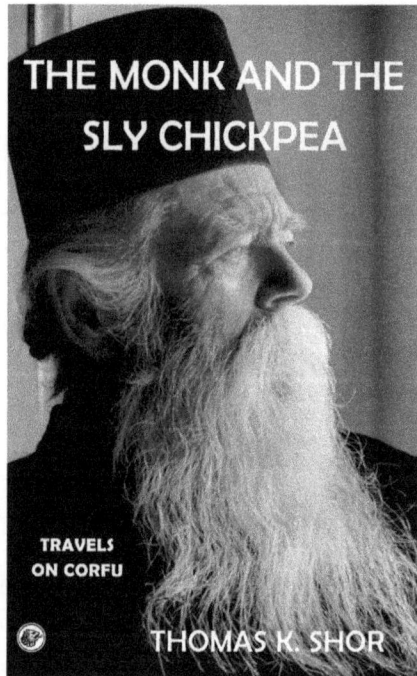

LEOPARD IN THE CITY
An Urban Fable
City Lion Press, 2018

A Leopard is Loose in the City!

LEOPARD IN THE CITY tells the tale of a leopard, a real leopard of the jungle, who suddenly finds himself in the center of a huge European city.

If seen, even by a single human being, he knows his fate would be sealed—either with a bullet through his heart or the sting of a tranquilizer gun, followed by a lifetime behind bars at the city zoo.

And who's to say which would be worse? In the zoo he would live out his days being gawked at as an anomaly, the famous mystery leopard from who-knows-where, the wild beast everybody read about in the newspapers, the one who disrupted life in the city and then was caught.

In order to avoid detection, he only moves about in the shadows deep in the night. Finding no edge to the city, no place where the city ends and the jungle begins, he sets himself the task of learning the ways of human beings. By understanding them he hopes to discover a loophole, a way out.

Befriended by a house cat, he comes to understand that long before human beings domesticated cats and dogs, they domesticated themselves: they tamed their own wild natures. It was by harnessing themselves that they were then able to harness nature's laws, which led ultimately to the engineering of skyscrapers and the angled grid of streets which appear to have no end, and through which the leopard is now forced to navigate.

Should he give up the dream of escape and follow the path of domestication as laid out by house cats, whose ancestors sacrificed their wild natures for security? Is it true, as house cats would have it, that the way to freedom is to submit willingly to domestication? Does way to salvation really lie in captivity? Does freedom come from in accepting subjugation? Is safety truly found not in liberty, but in the confinement, in the comfortable fate of a house cat living a privileged life of leisure with a secure place by the fire?

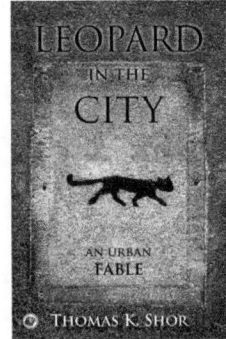

SCULPTURE GARDEN OF THE GODS

ANIMATED LANDSCAPE PHOTOGRAPHY FROM THE GREEK ISLAND OF IKARIA

City Lion Press, 2018

The Greek island of Ikaria has gained notoriety lately for being a so-called "Blue Zone," one of the select places on the planet where people live the longest. This otherwise obscure island was also known to the Ancients as the birthplace of the Greek god of ecstasy and wine, Dionysus, who was born upon the rocky ridge of mountain that runs down the center of the island.

SCULPTURE GARDEN OF THE GODS, a book of black and white photographs and prose, is the fruit of the author's three winters upon this mountain—often blown by hurricane-force winds and engulfed in thick fog.

Shor weaves the poetic force of his eye with that of his pen to take us on a journey to this otherworldly landscape, where lashing winds sculpt solid granite into forms that look like living beings with an uncanny regularity.

It is a place of mystery and beauty, where the most enduring is dissolved by the most fleeting, where wisps of fog blown by a gale can cause an entire mountain-side to disappear in an instant.

This book is also available in a bilingual English/Greek edition.

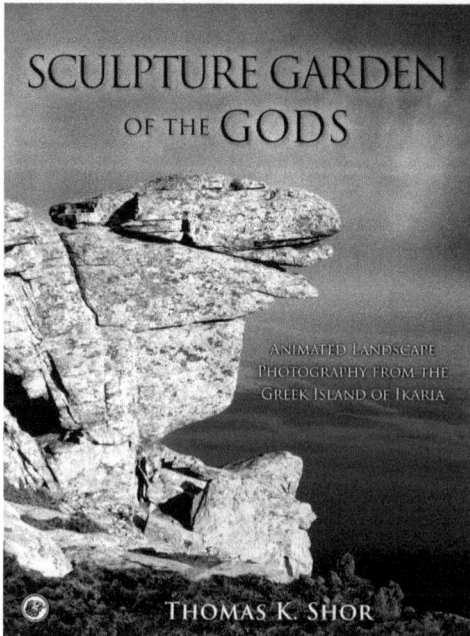

SCULPTURE GARDEN
OF THE GODS

ANIMATED LANDSCAPE
PHOTOGRAPHY FROM THE
GREEK ISLAND OF IKARIA

THOMAS K. SHOR

GANGES LAMENT

BLACK & WHITE PHOTOGRAPHIC PORTRAITS
FROM THE SACRED INDIAN CITY OF VARANASI

City Lion Press, 2018

These intimate portraits from the alleys close to the Ganges River were taken in winter when the river mist rose into the alleys, often persisting throughout the day. These alleys are among the oldest continuously inhabited places on the planet.

Varanasi is known as the City of Learning and Burning, referring both to the city's numerous schools, universities, ashrams, and pundits, as well as the many funeral pyres where faithful Hindus burn their dead by the river. Life and death are often juxtaposed in this chaotic and ancient city.

While the photographs portray people from all walks of life—and from differing faiths, ages, and social standing—they are mostly of people that others tend to consider outcasts and shy away from: the poor, street-dwellers, beggars, rickshaw pullers, widows discarded by their families, mourners with their shaved heads.

www.ingramcontent.com/pod-product-compliance
Ingram Content Group UK Ltd.
Pitfield, Milton Keynes, MK11 3LW, UK
UKHW040642171025
8435UKWH00003B/47

9 781957 890685